COMPUTER TERRORISM

Douglas E. Campbell, Ph.D.

COMPUTER TERRORISM

Direct all inquiries to Douglas Campbell at dcamp@syneca.com.

Cover design by Michelle Rekstad at Rekstad Graphics, rekstad@aol.com

Foreword

Nearly 20 years ago, in December 1992, I submitted this research in partial fulfillment of a requirement for my Doctor of Philosophy degree in Security Administration at Southwest University located in Kenner (New Orleans), LA.

The title of my research was initially called "Terrorist and Hostile Intelligence Actions Against Computer Resources;" the subtitle really explained it: A Detailed History of Terrorist and Hostile Intelligence Attacks Against Computer Resources and How to Reduce the Vulnerability of Such Attacks on Your Computer Center.

Much of what I said 20 years ago still rings true today: the proliferation of viruses and their use by foreign countries and in wartime situations comes to mind. Twenty years ago was also the age of the Rainbow Series of Department of Defense Computer Security Center manuals - the Red Book on *Trusted Network Interpretation*, the Orange Book on *Trusted Computer System Evaluation Criteria*, and some 20 other variously colored covers on everything dealing with computer security. This was pretty much all we had to work with at the time. I still believe the Orange Book is the de facto standard for computer security today as many National Institute of Standards and Technology (NIST) Special Publications and NIST Federal Information

Processing Standard (FIPS) Publications on computer security have followed in its footsteps.

So, with little editing, I am publishing my research to a wider audience in the hopes that it captures the attention of our younger computer scientists who may want to read what we thought of computer terrorism 20 years ago as compared to today, how much of the early efforts of computer security continue today and how one may prepare for a day when your computer center gets hacked.

Table of Contents

CHAPTER 1: NATURE OF THE PROBLEM

The problem is that terrorists, and terrorist organizations, are becoming more intelligent. Their use of technology is growing and their sophistication in terrorist actions has increased, as I will show. In the future, terrorist organizations may expand even further away from assassination, bombing, hijacking, and hostage taking and toward high-technology terrorism.[1] The Coordinator for Counterterrorism for the United States Department of State said "We anticipate that terrorists will make greater use of high technology in their attacks."[2]

The problem for the Security Administrator is that terrorists already realize that a small bomb or fire at a computer center can do more damage in a short amount of time than any other single event.

---

[1] David J. Icove, "Keeping Computers Safe," Security Management. December 1991, 30.

[2] Morris D. Busby, Coordinator for Counter-Terrorism, U.S. Department of State, from an address given to the International Seminar on Maritime and Port Security, Miami, Florida, January 3, 1990. The text was published by the U.S. Department of State Bureau of Public Affairs, Washington, D.C., in Current Policy No. 1243.

Terrorists have historically established a need to continue their destruction of computer resources. To date, "terrorists and activists have bombed more than 600 computer facilities. Terrorism is a pervasive threat against computer facilities worldwide."[3] Computers are rapidly becoming a favorite target for terrorists. "Already, terrorists have bombed hundreds of computer sites around the world."[4] Thus, most of this research paper is with establishing and validating the historical precedence.

Terrorism has been on the increase over the past eight years because of the availability of new targets. The term 'new targets' means that the vulnerabilities in advanced, open, industrial societies make suitable targets for terrorist attacks. These include large aircraft, supertankers, international power grids and pipelines, transportation hubs, commercial and communications centers, motorcades, offshore oil rigs, liquefied natural gas facilities, nuclear power facilities, and computerized information and management systems.[5] Computer centers are likely to be targets for future terrorists in the U.S. "Computer attacks already account for some 60 percent of all terrorist attacks in the world. It would be expensive and inconvenient to guard every office and factory, but some changes will have to be made to reduce their vulnerability to crippling terrorist attacks."[6]

---

[3] James Arlin Cooper, <u>Computer and Communications Security: Strategies for the 1990s</u> (New York: McGraw-Hill, 1989), 101.

[4] "Terrorism and Computers," <u>The Futurist</u>, January-February 1988, 45.

[5] Walter Laqueur and Yonah Alexander, <u>The Terrorism Reader: The Essential Source Book on Political Violence Both Past and Present</u>, (New York: Meridian Book, 1987), 279.

[6] Marvin Cetron, president of Forecasting International, Ltd., Arlington, VA, as quoted in "Terrorism: Home-Grown Threat to U.S.?" USA Today magazine, December 1989, 4.

Federal Bureau of Investigation (FBI) agent Neil Gallagher, who headed an antiterrorism unit in Boston, said in 1986: "Bombings against computer centers reached a peak last year, with 24 centers bombed in West Germany alone. What is frightening is that the more our society depends on computers, the greater the risk. The increasing reliance on computers for the normal operation of society has resulted in the creation of critical nodes whose destruction would be comparable to brain death. Thus we have greatly increased the potential for major disruption and economic loss stemming from sabotage of computer facilities or interference with computer operations."[7] Also, "a well-directed terrorist attack on 100 key computers could bring the American economy to a standstill."[8]   Winn Schwartau, Executive Director of International Partnership Against Computer Terrorism (Inter.Pact), has written a novel, Terminal Compromise, fictionalizing a series of devastating computer terrorist attacks against the United States.[9] He writes: "Computer terrorism provides the ideal mechanism for waging invisible remote control warfare, inflicting massive damage and leaving no tracks. Government policies and actions have created this country's most profound weakness: 70,000,000 computers, the mainstay of America's information society are virtually defenseless against invasion."   Fiction has already become fact.

In 1978 the Foreign Affairs Research Institute of London published a 10-page report on the problem of "intelligent terrorists" by Dominic Baron. It described how to cripple a

---

[7]Robert H. Kupperman and Darrell M. Trent, eds, Terrorism: Threat, Reality, Response, (Standford, CA, Hoover Institution Press, 1979), 8.
[8]Curtis J. Sitomer, "Crooks find computers useful; terrorists see vulnerable targets." The Christian Science Monitor. 4 December 1986, 6.
[9]Winn Schwartau, Terminal Compromise, (New York: Inter.Pact Press, 1991).

modern industrialized state by a terrorist attack on its computer systems. Clearly, Baron said, "access to major computing facilities will be open as much to the malefactor as to the good citizen, so it will not be difficult for the 'electronic terrorist' to use these facilities to plan optimal strategies for his attacks on the weakest points of some security system."[10]

The means of breaking into a computer are the same, whether for personal profit or destructive purposes. For example, a step-by-step description of a method used to divert goods is explained in one book.[11] The same method could be used by a terrorist group to steal weapons from an armory.

The problem is also that many self-proclaimed computer hackers are very intelligent and some of their actions should be considered terrorism. Terrorism through computers can be done in two ways: when the computer is the target and when it is the instrument of the operation. The first method would involve its destruction or temporary denial of use through, for example, sabotage. The second would involve altering or copying the data. It is the hacker who gets involved with the second scenario. Some hackers attack computer systems by either planting computer viruses or breaking in and stealing information--rather than just bombing the centers as traditional terrorists have done in the past. The number of computer viruses is increasing by 47 percent per year.[12] "At the rate things are going today, the "Carlos" of the future more likely will

---

[10]Richard C. Clark, Technological Terrorism, (Old Greenwich, CT: Devin-Adair Company, 1980), 163.

[11]Hsaio, Kerr and Madnick, Computer Security (New York: Academic Press, 1979), 98.

[12]National Computer Security Association, "Computer Viruses." 1 January 1991, 6.

be armed with an IBM PC than a Czech-made VZ61 machine pistol."[13]

The vulnerability of U.S. military systems was illustrated in 1988 when a group of West German hackers, using telephone lines, infiltrated a wide assortment of computers at U.S. military installations and corporations. Three men were convicted in February 1990 of selling some of that information--reportedly none of it classified--to the Soviet Union.[14] Perhaps the most blood-curdling threat to computer security is the vulnerability to terrorism found in most commercial information systems. Arguments by authorities [in the field of computer terrorism] have generally failed to draw much attention to the problem. As a form of intentional destruction, terrorism would seem to be the most pervasive and unpredictable. Terrorism can seem pervasive by applying levels of force beyond normal vandalism, industrial sabotage or burglary.[15]

The most recent problem is that terrorists themselves are using computers. Police raids on terrorist hideouts in South America, Europe and the Philippines have revealed that terrorists are also using computers, modems, and communications and database software. In a report released in December 1990, the National Academy of Sciences warned:

---

[13]Neil C. Livingstone, The Cult of Counterterrorism, (Lexington, MA: Lexington Books, 1990), 139. The "Carlos" referred to is Ilich Ramirez Savchez, better known as "Carlos the Jackal." He is one of the most infamous of all terrorists. The Czech-made Skorpion VZ61 submachine pistol is perhaps the most popular terrorist weapon in the world. "Carlos" carries a VZ61. Mr. Livingstone is president of the Institute on Terrorism and Subnational Conflict.

[14]Curt Suplee and Evelyn Richards, "Computers Vulnerable, Panel Warns," The Washington Post, 6 December 1990, A1.

[15]Richard Baskerville, Designing Information Systems Security, (New York: John Wiley & Sons, 1988), 14.

"Tomorrow's terrorist may be able to do more damage with a keyboard than with a bomb."[16]

Winn Schwartau states: "We don't normally think of the computer as a weapon. But in the wrong hands, our information processing systems can be turned against us."[17]

The overall problem is that terrorists are becoming more intelligent--where they once were smart enough to understand the damage that could be done through the destruction of computer resources belonging to others, they are now using computer technology to assist their causes. Modern electronics technology is providing terrorists with the means to create new variations on some of their oldest techniques: intimidation, kidnapping, murder and bombing. For example, modern digital electronics provides the ability to construct bombs with digital timers that can be set for a delay of weeks, months or years.[18] A computer chip found in the bomb wreckage of Pan Am Flight 103 at Lockerbie, Scotland, matched the configuration of electronic components of explosives seized in February 1988 from Libyan agents traveling in Senegal.[19] It is alleged that terrorists used a microprocessor to detonate the powerful bomb in Brighton, England, that almost killed Prime Minister Margaret

---

[16]Peter J. Ognibene, "America the Vulnerable," <u>Los Angeles Times</u>, 16 January 1991, B7.

[17]Winn Schwartau, "Seven Weapons for the Well-Armed Computer Terrorist," <u>Information Security Product News</u>, September/October 1991, 38.

[18]James W. Rawles, "High-Technology Terrorism," <u>Defense Electronics</u>, January 1990, 75.

[19]James Rowley, The Associated Press, "Libyans Indicted in Pan Am Blast. Pair Reportedly Intelligence Officers," <u>The Phoenix Gazette</u>, 14 November 1991, A3.

Thatcher. Four others lost their lives and more than 30 people were wounded. Technological terrorism is a growing problem.[20]

This is, I predict, a problem that will continue to escalate, and a very real problem if the Security Administrator does not take action to remain at least as computer-literate as the terrorists. The Security Administrator needs to remember that "In the tradition of spectacular heists, there's an element of art to the more clever computer-assisted thefts, with none of the heavy-handedness involved in marching into a bank toting a gun."[21]

An entire terrorist movement could be financed from the receipts of computer theft. Vital data could be stolen from computer information banks and ransomed back to the rightful owner.[22]

Purpose of My Research

The purpose of this research paper is to sensitize the Security Administrator to four major areas: the history of terrorist attacks against computer resources; on what intelligent hackers and viruses could do to the Security Administrator's computer resources; to make the Security Administrator sensitive to the fact that terrorists are also using computers and are becoming an increased threat because of their advancing intelligence of computer technology; and what mandatory minimum countermeasures the Security Administrator should put in place to protect his or her computer resources.

---

[20]August Bequai, Techno-Crimes: The Computerization of Crime and Terrorism (Lexington, MA: Lexington Books, 1987), 13.

[21]Lydia Dotto, "The New Computer Criminals," Atlas World Press Review. August 1979, 26.

[22]Neil C. Livingstone, The War Against Terrorism. (Lexington, MA: Lexington Books, 1982), 141.

Statement of the Hypotheses

Given that a hypothesis is an interpretation of a practical condition taken as grounds for action, I would like to bring a substantial number of applicable terrorist actions against computer resources under one document cover. Given that as a baseline, or the practical condition, my grounds for action would be the further discussion of the newest intelligent terrorist--the hacker--and how terrorists and hostile intelligence forces have used hackers for their own means. Building from there, I will demonstrate that terrorists themselves are using computer resources to assist in their terrorism. And finally, based on the author's own knowledge and experience, I will conclude with a listing of what I believe to be the mandatory minimum countermeasures to assist the Security Administrator in negating, as much as possible, the terrorist threat.

Rationale and Theoretical Framework of the Research

For the sake of argument, I would make a tentative assumption that there are thousands of American companies that have offices located in foreign countries. I would also make an assumption that the vast majority of these offices also contain computers and some even mainframe computer facilities. Given this, and adding to that list the U.S. Government military bases overseas, embassies, consulates, etc. (all of which have varying needs for computer resources), I would say that they all have someone responsible for protecting the equipment and data from malicious and accidental compromise. I tend to believe that the majority of these security personnel are not aware of the terrorist implications against their computers and data. In fact, Lawrence J. Fennelly, chief consultant to Assets Protection Training Institute, a security company, states it even better: "Part of the problem is that more than 60 percent of all corporations have no computer security programs whatsoever, and over half of these [corporations] have been ripped off."[23] As a Security Administrator, and given the above statements as my interpretation of a practical condition as grounds for my action, I desire to perform this research and show that the terrorist threat against computer resources exists, through historical evidence, and that terrorists are indeed becoming more intelligent as they themselves use computer technology. In short, terrorists and terrorism have entered the computer age and the Security Administrator must become more familiarize with what could happen to his or her computer resources.

Extent and Limitations of the Research

For the most part, companies do not wish to 'air their dirty laundry.' "Companies hit by computer crime believe that the less the public knows about their misfortunes, the better it is for business."[24] This was proven by the mass mailing of 418 letters requesting information from companies on terrorist attacks against their overseas branches. For the vast majority of responses, they declined to acknowledge that anything had ever happened to them. However, through third-party sources (books, newspapers, etc.), I found material to show that the damage and destruction of computer resources had historical precedence.

Other information was unavailable due to:

1. Current legal actions in which information could not be released. This was particularly true for companies that

---

[23]Curtis J. Sitomer, "Crooks find computers useful; terrorists see vulnerable targets." The Christian Science Monitor. 4 December 1986, 6.
[24]"Computer Crime Skeletons," Computerworld, November 29, 1982.

were legally entangled with taking hackers and ex-employees to court.

2. Corporate-sensitive information. Even Freedom of Information Act (FOIA) requests were of no use because only the Government is bound to FOIA, not the commercial world. Basically, competitive companies are not about to admit their shortcomings to the public.

3. Classified Department of Defense (DOD) data.

4. Current unavailability due to insurance reasons.

CHAPTER 2: REVIEW OF RELATED LITERATURE

My initial attempt to research related material was obtained through a mass mailing. Using a published directory of American firms operating in foreign countries, I found over 3,000 U.S. corporations which have over 22,500 subsidiaries and affiliates in 122 foreign countries.[25]   Of these 3,000 corporations, I mailed out 418 letters to the Foreign Operations Officer of those U.S. corporations that met the following criteria: More than 10,000 employees and that had American business activities in a foreign country other than Canada. The corporate standard for such mass mailing response is around 2-4 percent. I received 73 responses; a 17.5 percent response. However, even with the high response rate, not one company claimed to have had any terrorist actions taken against their computer resources in their foreign operations. Clearly, they underestimate the media in a free society: "IBM's offices in Dusseldorf were attacked in 1982. In June of that year, Control

---

[25]Directory of American Firms Operating in Foreign Countries. (New York: World Trade Academy Press, Volume I, 11th Edition, 1987).

Data Corporation's complex in Dusseldorf was blown up. That same month, one of McDonnell-Douglas's West German facilities was also hit. Two months later, in September 1982, Sperry's offices in West Berlin were the target of a terrorist raid. In December 1983, NCR's building in Vitoria and San Sebastian, Spain, were hit by terrorists. And Honeywell, whose offices in Athens were rocked by an explosion in 1981, came under another attack in July 1982, this time in Venice. In January of 1985, IBM's offices in West Berlin were bombed."[26]

Another source of related material came from electronic on-line searches through various databases in search of periodical and magazine articles on this research topic. My on-line research covered the following periodicals:

a. Arizona Republic, January 1991 - June 1992.
b. Atlanta Constitution, January 1985 - May 1992.
c. Boston Globe, January 1985 - May 1992.
d. Chicago Tribune, January 1985 - May 1992.
e. Christian Science Monitor, January 1985 - May 1992.
f. Dallas Morning News, January 1989 - June 1992.
g. The (Baltimore) Evening Sun, January 1990 - June 1992.
h. Los Angeles Times, January 1985 - May 1992.
i. New York Times, January 1987 - May 1992.
j. The Oregonian, January 1991 - June 1992.
k. St. Petersburg Times, January 1990 - May 1992.
l. Wall Street Journal, January 1985 - May 1992.
m. Washington Post, January 1989 - May 1992.
n. Washington Times, January 1991 - June 1992.

Another source of related material came from researching the Subject Guide to Periodicals.

---

[26] John Lamb and James Etheridge, "DP: The Terror Target," Datamation (February 1, 1986), 45. [Underline mine for emphasis only].

Other sources of related material came from library research at the Fairfax County, VA, library; The Richmond, VA, main library; the Fenwick Library on the campus of George Mason University; the Library of Congress, Washington, D.C.; The Federal Aviation Administration library; my personal library; and the American Society for Industrial Security (ASIS) library, of which I have been a member since 1984.

Finally, specific organizations assisted me in my research by providing me with articles which I could not locate elsewhere. These organizations included the Institute of Electrical and Electronics Engineers, Inc. (IEEE); and Interests, Ltd.

CHAPTER 3: RESEARCH FINDINGS

My research findings are divided into four sections. The first section, <u>The Destruction of Computer Resources By Terrorist Groups: An Historical Perspective</u>, is an historical look at incidents where terrorist groups have destroyed computer resources. By researching this particular area, I have proven that such incidents exist and that enough incidents have occurred to warrant concern on the part of the Security Administrator.

The second section, <u>Hackers and Hostile Intelligence Agents as Computer Terrorists</u>, is a look at how hackers have acted like terrorists in their actions to break in to computer centers or networks and either attempt to gather sensitive data off the networks or to plant computer viruses to destroy the data. This section also brings forth the facts that hostile enemy agents have used hackers to obtain sensitive U.S. information.

The third section, <u>Computer Resources Being Used By Terrorists</u>, is a look at the computer resources being used by terrorist groups. As an aside, I have included how the U.S. Department of Defense is also using computer terrorism techniques as a weapon, such as the introduction of a computer virus into an enemy's computer system.

The fourth and final section, <u>Methodology to Reduce the Vulnerability to Your Computer Center</u>, is what I consider to be the mandatory minimum requirements for the Security Administrator to implement against his or her computer resources to better protect those resources from a terrorist attack. These four sections are detailed as follows:

Section 1: The Destruction of Computer Resources By Terrorist Groups: An Historical Perspective.

> *"One of the aims of terrorists is to intimidate people by making them aware of their personal vulnerability. To a degree, they have been successful."*[27]

> *"Attacks on computers must escalate as society becomes more computer literate. Once terrorists wise up to the fact that a computer center is a sensitive part of a company, we can expect to see more of this kind of thing."*[28]

Since the early 1970s, numerous cases of physical attacks against foreign, U.S. government, and educational computer centers have been documented.[29] In the last decade, at least 57 computer centers in Europe, including six bank computer

---

[27]David E. Long, <u>The Anatomy of Terrorism</u>, (New York: The Free Press, 1990), ix.

[28]John Lamb and James Etheridge, "DP: The Terror Target," <u>Datamation</u> (February 1, 1986), 45. Article quotes Ken Wong, a security specialist with the British consulting firm BIS Applied Systems.

[29]Datapro Research Corporation, "Terrorism's Threat to Information Processing," July 1986.

centers, have been attacked by terrorists.[30] In certain countries, there is strong evidence that local terrorist groups are systematically trying to attack computers in industry and government. Our social fabric has become more critically dependent on the thread of technology as its binder. If this technology is fragile, it is an obvious terrorist target. As computer applications in many countries have become increasingly sophisticated, the operators of these systems have become increasingly concerned about the unforeseen consequences of total reliance on them.[31] There is no guarantee that computer facilities will continue to escape the notice of terrorists groups as an ideal target for the disruption of the basic structural elements of a society.[32] Indeed, one person has stated: "Based on material gathered and analyzed, the author estimates that by the end of 1982, over 100 terrorist attacks against computer targets of data processing personnel were committed. This estimate contradicts the general belief of those engaged with information systems' security, that the danger of terrorist attacks against those targets is low."[33] Since 1982, the attacks have continued. For example, at about 3 a.m. on Monday, September 2, 1985, two German software houses (Scientific Control Systems and Mathematischer Beratungs und Programmierungsdienst) had major computer center bombings within minutes of each other. The credited terrorist group

---

[30]Arnon Rozen and John Musacchio, "Computer Sites: Assessing the Threat," Security Management, July 1988, 41.

[31]L. Hoffman, "Impacts of Information System Vulnerabilities on Society," NCC Conference Proceedings (Arlington, VA: AFIPS Press, 1982).

[32]Belden Menkus, "Notes on Terrorism and Data Processing," Computers & Security, Vol. 2, January 1983, 11-15.

[33]R. Pollak, "Implications of International Terrorism on Security of Information Systems," Proceedings of IEEE INFOCOM 83 (New York: IEEE, 1983), 270-276.

considered the development of data processing systems as oppressive to workers.[34]

During a computer conference in Rome in 1986, it was claimed that more than 60 cases of serious acts of terrorism had been committed against computers or computer centers.[35] The following is an historical look at many of these incidents.

The Belfast Cooperative Society, Ltd., located in Ireland, had been using computers since 1948, starting with a Powers-Samas punch card and advancing to a Honeywell 200 system installed in 1967. Its data disks were stored in a Chubb fire protection safe.

The Society began backing up its data once a week when civil disturbances in Northern Ireland began escalating in 1971. The Society had a standing arrangement with Irish Hospitals Trust in Dublin for backup since its computer configurations were similar.

The computer room was located on the fourth floor of the building and was protected by a water sprinkler system, fire detection equipment, and a carbon dioxide fire suppression system. While members of the Society were prepared for a fire in the computer room, they failed to envision total destruction of the building by terrorist bombs.

---

[34]John Lamb and James Etheridge, "DP: The Terror Target," Datamation, February 1, 1986, 44-45.

[35]Stanley S. Arkin, et al, Prevention and Prosecution of Computer and High Technology Crime (New York, Matthew Bender & Co., 1992), Section 11.02[3][c]. The reference quotes its source as coming from page 94 of the International Computer Crime Proceedings (ICCP) Report entitled Computer-Related Crime: Analysis of Legal Policy, published by the Organization for Economic Cooperation and Development (OECD), Paris, 1986.

The first attack came in March 1972 when three armed men gained access to the building after overpowering the security guard. They placed one bomb on the first floor and one on the second. Only one exploded; the other was defused by demolition experts. A hole was blown in the second, but the company was able to place a barricade around it and proceed with business as usual.

However, on Wednesday, May 10, 1972, at 3:45 p.m., the company received a telephone call from a local newspaper. The newspaper reported that it had received a call from a person who claimed a bomb had been planted in the Society's building. Since the building was closed to the public on Wednesdays, the guard assumed that the only way the bomb could have gotten in was through the loading docks. Company personnel and police checked the receiving department and then searched the building.

With a limited number of people searching through a 300,000-sq.-ft. area, members of the group limited their search to looking for anything out of the ordinary. They found nothing. Since the company had been receiving an average of three telephone bomb threats per week, this threat was chalked up as just another hoax.

The bomb exploded at 4:40 p.m. on the second floor. The chief accountant, along with some of his people, rushed back to the office and went up though the building to the fourth floor where computer personnel were working. On the way up, they noticed a small fire on the second floor. However, the fire department was already on its way, so they passed the fire without fighting it.

Company personnel, and in particular computer center personnel, had practiced for such an event. When the chief accountant and his staff arrived, they found that the computer center personnel had remained calm, even though one of the punch card machines had been overturned by the force of the explosion. The staff had powered down the computer, put the tapes away, and locked the safe. The staff then walked across the flat roof and went down the fire escape stairway.

When the chief accountant went back into the building, he discovered that police were evacuating the building because they had received a call that a second bomb was about to go off. The building was sealed off at 4:50 p.m. At 5:15 p.m., heat from the enlarging fire began breaking the windows on the second floor. At 6:15 p.m., the building was an inferno

The fire department fought the fire for two days before it was brought under control, and by that time there was nothing left but a shell and some twisted metal. Ten days later the demolition crew found the company safe, which had fallen two floors down into the heart of the fire.

Forty tapes locked in the safe were recovered with minimal damage to only three tapes due to a blow torch which was used to burn off the hinges. However, the company had lost all its program listings and documentation, a number of transaction files had to be rerun, systems under development were a total loss, and manual operations were required for five weeks.[36]

---

[36]Adrian R.D. Norman, <u>Computer Insecurity</u>. (New York: Chapman and Hall, 1985), 117.

Computer centers in other parts of the world have also suffered terrorist attacks.

In a 30-month period between May 1976 and December 1978, the Red Brigades carried out bombing attacks against at least 10 computer centers located in Italy. The losses averaged about $1 million per attack. According to the statements made by the Red Brigades, the computer centers were singled out because they were 'instruments of the capitalist system' and must be destroyed. The Red Brigade manifesto specifically includes destruction of computer systems as an objective.[37] The attacks which were conducted by the Red Brigades are as follows:[38]

- May 1976. Five terrorists held employees at a Milan warehouse at gunpoint, set fire to the warehouse and destroyed the Honeywell computer center. At this time they called themselves "Movimento Armato Anti-Imperialista" or the "Anti-Imperialistic Military Movement." They left behind the following leaflet:

  "Today we have hit and destroyed another counter-revolutionary and anti-proletarian center of the government which stored information and names. We have shown the true face and the imperialistic design of the multinational Honeywell, engaged in the process of infiltration and leading to the center of data information of the bourgeois state. The power of the repressive and counter-revolutionary system is today

---

[37]Wallace S. Brushweiler, Sr., "Computers as Targets of Transnational Terrorism," Computer Security, Elsevier Science Publishers, North Holland, 1985.
      [38]Adrian R.D. Norman, Computer Insecurity. (New York: Chapman and Hall, 1985), 117.

based upon friendship and technical collaboration between the bourgeois apparatus and United States imperialism. Gendarmes, police and other uniformed slaves use the electronic information systems, in particular the Honeywell system. The methods have changed, the goals remain the same: yesterday the CIA system, today the multinationals. The target remains: exploitation and oppression. The chase after the imperialistic structure, until their successful destruction, is being continued by the militant forces. Smash and destroy the product of contrarevolution of the United States multinationals. We are building the movement of anti-imperialistic resistance!"[39]

- Also in May 1976, 15 men, armed with handguns and submachine guns, invaded a local government office in Rome and threw 10 Molotov cocktails among computer equipment installed there, destroying eight IBM 2740 terminals.[40]

- October 13, 1976. Plastic explosives destroyed the computer center at the De Angeli pharmaceutical firm in Milan.

- December 19, 1976. A number of security guards at Data-Montedison were tricked into opening a gate only to be overpowered by three men and a woman. These members of the Red Brigades explained that they were carrying birthday presents for an employee and that they wanted to

---

[39]Raoul Pollak, "Implications of International Terrorism on Security of Information Systems," IEEE INFOCOM 83, 272. Mr. Pollak is quoting his source as an internal report from the International Operations of Data Security Holdings, Inc.

[40]Thomas Whiteside, <u>Computer Capers: Tales of Electronic Thievery, Embezzlement, and Fraud</u>, (New York: Mentor Book, The New American Library, Inc.), 7.

come in and give him a surprise party. A communications controller was set on fire after being doused with gasoline. This one incident was given a closer look by another researcher, who depicts much larger destruction at the hands of the terrorists:

"Terrorists attacked the computer center of a multi-national company. The computer center was housed in a building in an industrial area separated from other offices of the company. Access was controlled by a uniformed guard and electronically operated doors into the facility. The well-dressed individuals explained to the guard that they had a surprise birthday party planned for one of the computer operators and were carrying a number of large boxes wrapped as gifts. The guard admitted them to the lobby and asked to inspect the contents of the boxes. At that point, the individuals opened the boxes, removed automatic weapons, incapacitated the guard temporarily, and entered the computer center. They forced all of the employees in the computer center at gunpoint into the lobby, where they were temporarily held. The entire computer center, including the tape library and programming office, was drenched with gasoline. A fuse was set at the main entrance. The attackers fled in cars, the employees left the building, and the building exploded and burned, completely destroying its contents."[41]

---

[41]Donn B. Parker, Manager's Guide to Computer Security, (Reston, VA: Reston Publishing Co., Inc., 1981), 296.

- January 17, 1977. At the Sias steel manufacturing plant, a bomb placed above a computer center damaged the IBM 370/135 on the floor below.

- April 15, 1977. Four armed terrorists forced their way into the Liquechimica petrochemical company in Calabria, doused a production control center with gasoline and set it on fire.

- April 21, 1977. A man and two women forced their way into the University of Bocconi, Milan, computer center and blew up computer equipment.

- June 10, 1977. A three-woman team broke into the University of Rome computer center and destroyed a Univac 1110. The masked women carried Uzi submachine and silencer-equipped hand guns. While holding two professors and an assistant hostage, they allowed all other personnel to evacuate the building. They then poured gasoline on the center's computer and set fire to it. Damage to the computer and the premises was estimated at more than $2-$4 million.[42]

- July 1978. Seven armed terrorists attacked a computer center in Turin and set it on fire with Molotov cocktails. The employees were locked up but managed to escape.

- July 15, 1978. "Red Brigades destroyed a regional computer center in Torrino."[43]

---

[42]Thomas Whiteside, <u>Computer Capers: Tales of Electronic Thievery, Embezzlement, and Fraud</u>, (New York: A Mentor Book, The New American Library, Inc. 1978), 7.

[43]Raoul Pollak, "Implications of International Terrorism on Security of Information Systems," IEEE INFOCOM 83, 274. Mr. Pollak is quoting from an internal report produced by the International Operations of Data Security Holdings, Inc.

- December 3, 1978. At 6:00 a.m., the computer center at the Italian Ministry of Transport in Rome (Motorizzazione Civile) was bombed and set on fire. Three armed men broke in, with the complicity of one of the employees. They bound and gagged the two operators and poured gasoline over the equipment. The resultant fire destroyed the dual Honeywell Level 66 systems which held the records of all Italian cars, stolen cars and false license plates. Eugenio Orlandi states in his research paper <u>Data Processing Security and Terrorism</u> that "When the terrorists concentrated in destroying computers they tested the high vulnerability of a virtually defenceless society. The bombs and fire did not invest all the disk units and the offices. It was possible to restore the site ... from previous general saves, partially destroyed disks, reports."[44] However, this incident destroyed so much data that nearly two years passed before the ministry had any reasonable idea of who in the country owned cars and trucks or had licenses to drive them. A Reuters newswire report stated that "hundreds of thousands of files and microfilms representing more than 20 million documents were destroyed."[45]

The Red Brigades, also called The Armed Anti-Imperialist Movement, the Anti-Imperialistic Military Movement (MAA), Communist Unity Fighters, the Armed Communist Formation, the Communist Combat Unit, and the Proletarian Patrols, announced their strategies and goals against computer centers

---

[44]Eugenio Orlandi, "Data Processing Security and Terrorism," a paper given at the Second International Federation for Information Processing (IFIP) International Conference on Computer Security, Toronto, Canada, 10-12 September, 1984.

[45]Reuters newswire dispatch dated December 3, 1978, as quoted by Richard C. Clark, <u>Technological Terrorism</u>, (Old Greenwich, CT: Devin-Adair Company, 1980), 162.

in their February 1978 publication entitled "Risoluzione Della Direzione Strategica" or "Red Brigades Strategic Direction Resolution." This 80-page publication describes the rationale behind, in part, the destruction of computer centers.

The Red Brigades have identified multinational corporations (mostly those with ties to the United States which explains the large number of U.S.-built computers destroyed by the Red Brigades) as their enemy. They have identified computers in a two-fold manner: 1) As the foremost instruments of the ability of multinationals to succeed, and 2) As the most dangerous instruments to be used against them in terms of files and cross-referencing. To quote a paragraph from their publication: "...we find the organizing of a European computer-filing system centralizing all information on guerrilla groups; on the militant members, on their methods; centralizing all data relative to kidnappings, numbers of banknote's series, etc."

The heart of the publication as it concerns computer centers and computer technology is as follows:

> "We must not underestimate the use of computer technology in the repression of the class war, as the efficiency of computers is supported by the ideology and by the technical-military personnel responsible for their functioning.

> "Computer systems are the monopoly of the American multinationals and, in addition to ensuring the United States hegemony over the world economy (the electronic sector is the strategic sector of advanced capitalism), they also guarantee the exportation of forms of control, of police methods, and they export also the highest levels of repression, ripened in the strongest link of imperialism. In fact, the exportation of

these "systems" is not only exportation of advanced technology, it is also a relationship of production, of an ideology. It is the American "filing system" ruling the control structures of all the states of the imperialistic chain. And exactly because of this, it is also the creation of a layer of technicians-policemen in charge of preventive and total espionage of the people. You see, computers are identified as a symbol, the highest profile target. It is important to destroy their mesh, to disrupt these systems, beginning from the technical-military personnel which directs them, instructs them, and makes them functional against the proletariat."[46]

Of interest is the computer center bombed in Frankfort, Germany. The computer center actually belonged to a U.S. Army intelligence facility. A terrorist group calling itself In the Heart of the Beast took credit, proclaiming, "Death to U.S. imperialism."[47]

The United States is also included when it comes to computer terrorism. In November 1969, five members of an anti-war group calling itself "Beaver 55" attacked a chemical company's Hewlett-Packard computer center in Midland, Michigan. One thousand tapes were damaged with small magnets. It was a long and expensive job to recreate the files--damage was estimated at $100,000. Attacking a centralized

---

[46]Raoul Pollak, "Implications of International terrorism on Security of Information Systems," Proceedings of the IEEE INFOCOM 83, 271. Mr. Pollak is quoting his source as coming from an internal report belonging to the International Operations of Data Security Holdings, Inc. Mr. Pollak is the Chairman of the Information Security Committee, E.D.P. Auditors Association, Israel.

[47]August Bequai, Techno-Crimes: The Computerization of Crime and Terrorism, (Lexington, MA: Lexington Books, 1987), 132.

source of information was a way to both protest and sabotage U.S. involvement in the Vietnam War.[48]   The terrorists thought they had destroyed data from research into such areas as nerve gases, napalm, defoliants, and other secret chemical weapons. What they had in fact destroyed were records of the local blood bank, research on air pollution, history of the company's industrial health program, and the chemical test results of a mumps vaccine under development. Again in Michigan, in Eagan this time, saboteurs broke into a Sperry Corporation plant and destroyed military computer equipment that was to be used for nuclear weapons guidance and control systems.[49]

In 1969 and 1970, computer centers were also attacked at Boston University, California's Fresno State College, and the University of Kansas.   In March 1976 a Hewlett-Packard electronic circuit manufacturing site in Palo Alto, California, was bombed. And in May 1976 bombs were exploded in two floors of a Kennebec building housing the data processing facilities of Central Maine Power. One Vietnam War protest action inside the Pentagon did involve the bombing of an unoccupied restroom. Water from the damaged plumbing lines reportedly flooded and disabled a nearby classified U.S. Air Force computer center.[50]   Further research revealed that the incident did indeed disable the computer center; the restroom was located directly above the computer center on the next floor.

In 1970, American anti-war activists set off a bomb outside the Army Mathematics Research Center at the University of

---

[48]Jay Bloombecker, ed., Introduction to Computer Crime (Los Angeles, CA: National Center for Computer Crime Data, 1985), 109.
[49]August Bequai, Techno-Crimes: The Computerization of Crime and Terrorism, (Lexington, MA: Lexington Books, 1987), 135.
[50]Belden Menkus, "Notes on Terrorism and Data Processing," Computers & Security, January 1983, 13.

Wisconsin. The blast killed Robert Fassnacht, a 30-year-old postdoctoral researcher working there after hours. Damage included a Control Data Corporation 3600 system, a Univac 9300 terminal, a Honeywell DDP124 and a Scientific Control Corporation 4700 computer. Three smaller computers belonging to the physics department were also destroyed. The explosion damaged 10 buildings (mainly by shattering window glass). What was believed to be the world's finest cryogenic (extremely low temperature) lab was also destroyed and subsequently all projects, including those in the field of superconductivity, were abandoned. It was estimated that the research data represented 1.3 million staff hours of effort built up over 20 years. The loss was estimated at more than $18 million. The complete story of this incident can be read in Tom Bates' Rads.[51]

On September 28, 1973, "a time bomb demolished four rooms in the Latin American Section of International Telephone and Telegraph (ITT) Corporation headquarters in New York, but no one was injured. The attack was linked to the radical Weatherman faction of the (SDS, Students for a Democratic Society), connected with Al Fatah, PFLP (Arab terrorist organizations), and the IRA (Irish Republican Army). The bombing, which coincided with several bomb blasts elsewhere in the world, was reported to be a protest against ITT's activities in Chile."[52]

In March 1984, a U.S. terrorist group calling themselves United Freedom Front bombed an IBM facility in White Plains,

---

[51]Tom Bates, Rads: The 1970 Bombing of the Army Math Research Center at the University of Wisconsin and its Aftermath, (New York: HarperCollins Publishers, 1992).

[52]International Terrorism: A Chronology, 1968-1974," a report prepared for the Department of State by the Defense Advanced Research Projects Agency (DARPA). (Santa Monica, CA: The Rand Corporation, March 1975), 49.

New York. They claimed that the attack was in protest of the company's business operations in South Africa.[53]

In a publicly distributed newsletter, the group claimed that "IBM is a death merchant ... The computer is an integral part of the fascist South African government's policies of racist repression and control."[54] Another attack on a computer center in South Africa resulted in one fatality:

> "Durban Oct 2 SAPA--A young computer consultant who recently completed his national service was killed instantly when he opened a parcel bomb at his offices in Durban on Tuesday [2 Oct] morning.
>
> "The explosion rocked the premises of PC Plus Consultants, a computer hardware and service company, at 37 Crart Avenue at 9.20AM [0720 GMT].
>
> "The bomb box was delivered by a transport company and was thought to have contained a computer in need of repairs. It exploded as the parcel was opened by Mr. Nic Cruse, aged about 23, according to the co-owner of PC Plus, Mr. Tam Alexander. Mr. Cruse, who had been employed by PC Plus only since August 1, was killed instantly.
>
> "The bomb extensively damaged an office in the residential house converted into business premises. Two front windows and steel burglar bars were blown completely out of the window frame. Police were on the scene almost immediately and the area was

---

[53]Datapro Research Corporation, "Terrorism's Threat to Information Processing," July 1986.
[54]John Lamb and James Etheridge, "DP: The Terror Target," Datamation (February 1, 1986), 45.

cordoned off as detectives combed the area. Residents living across the road said they heard a tremendous explosion followed by a woman's scream.

"Mr. Alexander suggested the bombing might have been politically motivated because his company supplied merchandise to 'liberal organisations.' Recent clients included the ANC [African National Congress], Women for Peaceful Change, the Black Sash and trade unions. Several of the company's employees were also ANC members, Mr. Alexander said.

"Police confirmed the death but said further details were unavailable. Crart Avenue is in a busy residential sector with a nursery school nearby.

"Mr. Alexander said the company had experienced 'political problems' some time ago, but he had not believed they would result in death. He did not elaborate but said the bomb had come without warning. Another employee, Mr. Gary Pelser, said he had recently clashed with members of a rightwing organisation and had received threatening letters at his home. 'I wouldn't put it past them to do something like this,' he said."[55]

Canada has also suffered destruction of their computers at the hands of terrorists. In February 1969, rioting students

---

[55]Foreign Broadcast Information Service (FBIS) message traffic, "Durban Bomb Fatality at Computer Center." FBIS source came from a Johannesburg, South Africa SAPA broadcast in English on October 2, 1990, at 1229 GMT.

burned the computer center at Montreal's Sir George Williams University.[56]

A long battle of terrorist groups against computer centers was also occurring in France. On August 14, 1979, at the Bank de Rothschild in Paris, windows of the keypunching room were blown out and data processing facilities were attacked with Molotov cocktails, causing major damage in the data preparation area.[57]

In Toulouse, France, on 20 May 1980, an organized left-wing terrorist group calling itself the Comite Liquidant ou Detoumant les Ordinateurs (Committee on the Liquidation or Deterrence of Computers--CLODO. 'Clodo' is also French slang for 'tramp.') and a terrorist group calling itself the "Direct Action Organization of March 27-28" claimed responsibility for the destruction of computer systems and data during an attack on Philips Data Systems. Another report translated CLODO as "Computer Liquidation and Hijacking Committee."[58] Still another translated CLODO as "Committee for the Liquidation and Misappropriation of Computers."[59] And still another claims CLODO stands for "Committee for Releasing or Setting Fire to Computers."[60] Processed World, an underground magazine published in the United States, reprinted a rare interview with a representative of CLODO in its 10th issue.

---

[56]Belden Menkus, "Notes on Terrorism and Data Processing," Computers & Security, January 1983, 13.

[57]Donn B. Parker, "Computer Abuse, Perpetrators and Vulnerabilities of Computer Systems," a paper prepared for the National Science Foundation, Washington, D.C.

[58]Christopher Dobson and Ronald Payne, Counterattack: The West's Battle Against the Terrorists. (New York: Facts on File, Inc., 1982), 182.

[59]Time-Life editors, Computer Security, (Alexandria, VA: Time-Life Books), 40.

[60]Adrian R.D. Norman, Computer Insecurity, (New York: Chapman and Hall, 1985), 230.

Philips specializes in the sale of computers and the storage of bookkeeping data of private companies. The terrorists claimed to have destroyed the equipment and data because, according to the terrorists, the equipment and data were being used by the armed forces and the French counter-espionage organization.

Members of the two terrorist organizations gathered the computer programs and magnetic data cards and burnt them in the toilets of the offices. They also damaged the computers and removed all the personnel files from the firm.

In a statement by CLODO to the left-wing newspaper 'Liberation,' it said: "We are computer workers and therefore well placed to know the present and future dangers of computer systems. Computers are the favorite instrument of the powerful. They are used to classify, to control and to repress. We do not want to be shut up in ghettos of programs and organizational patterns."[61] A different translation of the statement was published in another magazine: "We are workers in the field of data processing and consequently well placed to know the current and future dangers of data processing and telecommunications. The computer is the favorite tool of the dominant. It is used to exploit, to put on file, to control, and to repress."[62]

As if to help the terrorists make their point, the pro-government daily newspaper Le Figaro pointed out, "the destruction of a computer could cause far more damage than

---

[61]August Bequai, Techno-Crimes: The Computerization of Crime and Terrorism, (Lexington MA: Lexington Books, 1987), 129.

[62]John Lamb and James Etheridge, "DP: The Terror Target," Datamation (February 1, 1986), 44.

the murder of a politician."[63]   Another source states that the newspaper wrote: "...a modern nation is infinitely vulnerable. It is much more effective for those who aim to harm or even paralyze it to put computers out of action than to shoot up ministries or murder policemen."[64]

Within four days of the attack on Philips, the computer center for the CII-Honeywell-Bull company in Toulouse was set on fire. Soon after, responsibility was claimed by the same "Direct Action Organization" group in a telephone call to the French press agency. The caller told the press that a systematic plan to paralyze the operations of computer firms located in France was in operation. Their group was out to destroy computer systems on the grounds that they were weapons in the hands of the government. The other group, CLODO, also claimed responsibility. CLODO had approached both Philips and CII-Honeywell-Bull earlier when it had placed bombs at the computer centers. There was no damage and CLODO made its involvement public by scrawling slogans on the grounds proclaiming "Out With Computers."

In June 1980, CLODO terrorists in Toulouse ransacked a hall which had been prepared for an international symposium. The raiders left the message: "Scientist swine. 'No' to capitalist data processing."

Around the same time, another band of French terrorists, picking up CLODO's computer cudgel, fired a bazooka rocket at the buildings that housed the French Ministry of Transportation in Paris. The "Action Directe," which claimed credit for the

---

[63]Christopher Dobson and Ronald Payne, <u>Counterattack: The West's Battle Against the Terrorists</u>. (New York: Facts on File, Inc., 1982), 183.
    [64]Andrew Lloyd, "DP: An Easy Target," <u>Datamation</u> (June 1, 1980), 100.

attack, wanted to protest the agency's 'planned computer projects,' Its salvo of protest, however, missed its mark. Instead of landing as planned on the sixth floor computer center, the explosive ended up in the library one floor below. The blast was intended to dramatize "Action Directe's" doctrine that computers, used as instruments of repression by the government, condemn people to the 'ghettos of program and organizational patterns.'[65]

On 11 December 1980, the French magazine Computer Weekly reported:

Bomb Attacks on French Centres

"French police are bracing themselves for a new wave of fire bomb attacks on computers following the recent blaze at a central Paris office building owned by a major insurance company. Computers housed in the basement of a seven-storey block near the opera house were undamaged by the fire, which spread to the roof where five office workers were rescued by the fire brigade. Police evacuated 600 people from the burning building during the evening rush hour. A few minutes later, an anonymous telephone caller claimed responsibility for the outbreak on behalf of the self-styled 'CLODO' movement which was answerable for a long catalogue of attacks on computers.

"CLODO, a slang term for 'tramp,' stands for Comite de Liberation Ou de Detournement des Ordinateurs (Committee for Releasing or Setting Fire to Computers). The organisation first made newspaper

---

[65]John Lamb and James Etheridge, "DP: The Terror Target," Datamation (February 1, 1986), 44.

headlines last April when it placed bombs at the Toulouse computer centres operated by Philips Informatique and CII-Honeywell-Bull. There was no damage and CLODO made its involvement known by scrawling slogans proclaiming 'Out with computers.'

"CLODO emerged again on May 20 when it burned down ICL's shop, again in Toulouse. Computer wreckers returned to the attack in the same city on June 25 when they ransacked a hall which had been prepared for an international symposium. The raiders left behind the message "Scientist swine. No to capitalist data processing.'

"CII-Honeywell-Bull's centre at Louveciennes, near Paris, was singled out in August for a series of attacks. First, a ten-pound plastic bomb was left outside the wall of the buildings but failed to detonate. Then a security door protecting computers and confidential software was destroyed, police finding next day a one-foot deep hole bored in a wall, apparently for a future explosive charge.

"CLODO switched its attention back to Toulouse on September 12 when three fires gutted a computer and electronics goods shop."[66]

On 23 March 1981, terrorists struck again, this time destroying an IBM computer at the local headquarters of the Banque Populaire in Toulouse. They broke into the computer center through a window and actually set off an automatic

---

[66]"Bomb Attacks on French Centres," Computer Weekly, 11 December 1980.

alarm. However, they still had time to damage the computer, a terminal, and a line-printer before escaping.

In May 1981, another computer center in Toulouse was seriously damaged in a bomb attack. "British Power Kills in Ireland" was scrawled on the walls of the building. None of the residents were hurt in the dawn explosion but stores and equipment were destroyed. Despite the IRA slogan, police believe CLODO was responsible.

The 1983 bombing attack against the West German Maschinenfabrick Ausburg-Nuernberg (MAN) computer center was an act committed by terrorists calling themselves Rote Zellen in order to protest against the participation of the MAN Company in the production of Pershing and Cruise missiles and transportation systems. Damages to the center exceeded $7 million; however it would have been much more had the back-up copies of the data in the computer system also been destroyed (they were located at another site).[67] The group warned that additional attacks would follow if the company didn't cease manufacturing transport vehicles for the missiles.

In October 1984, a new terrorist group literally exploded onto the European terrorism stage with a series of bombings. These bombings included sites that had been the previous bombing targets of other terrorist organizations. In October 1984, the Combatant Communist Cells (Cellules Communistes Combattantes, or CCC), headed by Pierre Carrette, bombed the headquarters of Litton Data Systems in Brussels and severely damaged three buildings and 25 vehicles. Also during October

---

[67]Ulrich Seiber, The International Handbook on Computer Crime: Computer-related Economic Crime and the Infringements of Privacy, (New York: John Wiley & Sons, 1986), 15. According to Seiber's own footnote, this case description was based on police and company statements.

they bombed the parking lot of the MAN Corporation, the headquarters of Honeywell-Bull, and the computerized Belgian Liberal Party Research Center, all in the Brussels, Belgium, area.

> "Brussels, October 15 -- A bomb seriously damaged a research centre linked with the Liberal Party early today, in the fourth bombing in the Belgium capital in two weeks. First accounts said a man hurled a bomb into the ground floor of the building and escaped in a car. Damage was severe, and windows were shattered in a dozen nearby buildings. The attack was not immediately claimed.

> "Since October 2 a previously unknown "Communist Combatant Cell" has claimed bomb attacks against three companies involved in projects for the North Atlantic Treaty Organization (NATO) here: Litton, Man and Honeywell. Belgium's Liberal deputy premier, Jean Gol, was particularly severe in his condemnation of these attacks."[68]

The Belgium terrorist group CCC is believed to have joined with the West German Red Army Faction (RAF) and the French group Direct Action (AD) in forming an Anti-Imperialist Armed Front to conduct attacks to protest the "Americanization of Europe" and to frustrate increased military cooperation among members of NATO.[69] Other destructive efforts took place:

---

[68]Foreign Broadcast Information Service, "Research Center Damaged in Bomb Explosion," FBIS message traffic quoted from Paris source given in English at 0752 GMT on 15 October 1984.
[69]Terrorist Group Profiles, (Washington, D.C.: Government Printing Office), November 1988, 41.

- November 21, 1984 - Brussels, Belgium. Offices of the U.S. electronic company Motorola are bombed. The Belgium terrorist group Communist Combattant Cells (CCC) claims responsibility. It was reported that the terrorist group left a note that delivered the kind of ultimatum that computer firms and users are beginning to dread: "This is a revolutionary action against the Motorola offices. In the interests of your security, leave the building immediately. It will be destroyed 30 minutes after one of our militants has taken action." While the building wasn't seriously actually destroyed, it was seriously damaged.[70]

- November 26, 1984 - Liege, Belgium. Two military communications masts at a NATO base near Liege are destroyed by a bomb. CCC claims responsibility.

- December 6, 1984 - Oudenarde, Belgium. A bomb explodes at a NATO fuel pumping station in central Belgium. CCC claims responsibility.

- December 6, 1984 - Paris, France. A bomb explodes at the offices of NATO's Central European Operating Agency, near Versailles outside Paris, which manages the 5,900 kilometer NATO pipeline network. CCC claims responsibility but also states that an unspecified "international communist group in France" assisted.

- December 11, 1984 - Verviers, Belgium. Six bombs simultaneously explode along NATO's emergency fuel pipeline near Brussels, forcing a temporary shutdown of computerized operations. CCC claims responsibility stating that it is fighting a "war against NATO."

---

[70]John Lamb and James Etheridge, "DP: The Terror Target," Datamation (February 1, 1986), 45.

- December 30, 1984 - Mannheim, FRG. A U.S. Army communications center is bombed. RAF claims responsibility.

- January 3, 1985 - Heidelberg, FRG. A bomb explodes at a molecular biology center at Heidelberg University. RAF claims responsibility.

- In January 1985 the CCC bombed a NATO support facility in suburban Brussels.

- January 15, 1985 - Paris, France. France's Action Directe (AD) and the RAF release a five-page statement announcing the start of joint operations targeted at NATO.

- January 21, 1985 - Stuttgart, FRG. A known RAF sympathizer, Johannes Thimme, is killed and his female companion is seriously injured when a bomb they were wheeling in a baby carriage toward a computer center explodes prematurely.

- April 30, 1985 - Paris, France. Two telecommunications firms connected with the French arms industry are bombed. AD claims responsibility.

- August 15, 1985 - Wuppertal, FRG. Branch of the U.S.-based Westinghouse Corporation at Wuppertal, north of Cologne, is bombed.

- November 16, 1985 - Heidelberg, FRG. IBM computer research center sustains serious damage from a bomb attack.[71]

---

[71]Randall Heather, Terrorism, "Active Measures", and SDI, (Toronto, Canada: The Mackenzie Institute for the Study of Terrorism, Revolution and Propaganda, 1987)

The bombings in late August-early September 1985 were particularly severe.

> "Bombs caused nearly $1.5 million in damage to two West German computer companies with military contracts, officials reported. Police said no one was hurt, and there were no immediate claims of responsibility. The affected companies are a subsidiary of the Hoesch Steel firm in Dortmund which has sold a computer program to the U.S. Army, and Scientific Control Systems in Hamburg, which is owned by British Petroleum."[72]

In December 1985, the CCC exploded a bomb at the Bank of America offices, causing major damage to the building, to the computers, and to the surrounding area. In December 1985, Pierre Carrette and three other CCC militants were arrested and no known CCC attacks have since occurred.

Recently, the RAF was blamed for a series of bombings on computer centers, including the Frankfurt, Germany, Stock Exchange:

> "Assailants hurled firebombs inside the Frankfurt Stock Exchange and an electronics firm Wednesday [April 12, 1989], and police blamed both attacks on supporters of jailed terrorists staging a hunger strike.
>
> "Authorities said the attacks destroyed or damaged several computers and delayed the opening time by a few minutes.
>
> "Authorities said the attack caused millions of dollars worth of damage but no injuries.

---

[72]"The World," Los Angeles Times, 3 September 1985, 2.

"Earlier, in the northern city of Muenster, unidentified assailants set off a firebomb inside the offices of the AEG electronics firm, a subsidiary of the Daimler-Benz automotive and high-technology conglomerate."[73]

In an April 1987 example, a bomb exploded and damaged a decoding computer plant in Bavaria"

"Tutzing, West Germany, April 13 -- A bomb exploded Sunday night in the basement of a Bavarian computer plant specializing in the production of decoding devices used by security services, police said Monday. Police estimated the damage to the plant at between six and eight million Deutsche marks (between 3.3 and 4.4 million dollars). A witness said he saw two young men fleeing from the building on foot shortly after the explosion. Investigators have not ruled out the possibility that the two were wounded in the attack. TST TeleSecurity, based in the neighbouring community of Poecking, has its production plant in this Bavarian town, on the perimeter of Lake Sternberg. It mainly manufactures devices used to decode and analyze handwriting. Bavarian police have not ruled out a political motive behind the bombing, and are offering a reward of 5,000 marks (2,800 dollars) for information leading to the capture of the criminals. Computer firms with large

---

[73]Associated Press editors, "West German Attack Tied to Pro-Terrorists," The Atlanta Journal and Constitution, 13 April 1989, 35A.

defence contracts have in the past few years been the targets of several bomb attacks in West Germany."[74]

Although the above report states that the company affected "mainly manufactures devices used to decode and analyze handwriting," another report was a bit more specific:

"13 April 1987, Munich FRG. A bomb explodes at the Munich office of TST, a computer firm that does business with West German security and intelligence agencies, specializing in cryptographic equipment."[75]

Even in a quiet part of the world, computers are being destroyed, as evidenced from this article coming from Malta:

"Valletta, Oct 13 1984 -- A bomb wrecked a computer used by 19 Maltese Government departments today and caused 1.5 million dollars' worth of damage, informed sources said here. The explosion was at a government electronics centre at Dingli, 13 kilometers (eight miles) from Valletta, and responsibility has not been claimed.

"The sources said the bombers cut a hole in wire fencing and slipped past two security guards before placing the device at the window of the room where the computer was kept. The electronics centre was

---

[74]Foreign Broadcast Information Service, "Bomb Damages Decoding Computer Plant in Bavaria," FBIS message traffic quoted from source in Paris in English at 1244 GMT on April 13, 1987.

[75]Randall Heather, Terrorism, "Active Measures", and SDI, (Toronto, Canada: The Mackenzie Institute for the Study of Terrorism, Revolution and Propaganda, 1987), 30.

opened three years ago in a building formerly used by the British Navy."[76]

Computers have also been destroyed elsewhere in the world. For example, members of the East Asian Anti-Japan Front made their way into the ninth-floor offices of a Japanese construction company and planted a bomb that seriously damaged the company's computer system. And in England, members of a group calling itself "Angry Brigade" attempted to bomb police computers in London.[77]

Also in London, animal rights activists are being called terrorists by the British government after the activists claimed responsibility for a bomb that blew up at the University of Bristol and severely damaged the university's computer center:

> "Two animal rights groups in Britain have claimed responsibility for a bomb that caused severe damage to the administration block at the University of Bristol. The activists said that the high-explosive device was intended to be a protest against research using animals being carried out at the university's medical and veterinary schools.

> "Although militant animal rights groups have, in recent years, admitted responsibility for a number of incendiary devices planted in stores in London and elsewhere, the Bristol University blast is the first time that high explosives have been used in such incidents.

---

[76]Foreign Broadcast Information Service, "Government Computer Destroyed in Bomb Explosion," FBIS message traffic quoted from source in Paris in English at 1543 GMT 13 October 1984.
[77]August Bequai, Technocrimes: The Computerization of Crime and Terrorism (Washington, D.C.: Lexington Books, 1987).

"There were no casualties in the explosion, which took place in the early hours of 23 February [1989]. However, the bomb caused severe damage to a bar and dining area used by university teaching and research staff, as well as the to the university's computer.

"After visiting the scene of the explosion, the British Secretary of State for Education and Science, Kenneth Baker, described it as 'an act of terrorism.'[78]

In the United States, saboteurs made four attempts to damage the computer center at the Wright-Patterson Air Force Base near Dayton, Ohio.[79]

To date, terrorists have bombed hundreds of computer sites around the world.[80] These actions are fast replacing kidnapping or assassinations of political and business leaders as a means to have their demands met or at least publicized. When a terrorist group or other organization has a point of view it wants to receive public attention, it may sabotage a computer instead of kidnapping the head of the company.[81]

Terrorist propaganda that often accompanies such destruction focuses on the computer as a symbol or as an instrument of capitalistic oppression. August Bequai, a Washington, D.C., attorney and an expert in the field of terrorism, describes the computer as a symbol:

---

[78]David Dickson, "Animal Rightists Claim Bomb Blast," Science, March 3, 1989, 1133.

[79]August Bequai, Techno-Crimes: The Computerization of Crime and Terrorism, (Lexington MA: Lexington Books, 1987), 130.

[80]"Terrorism and Computers," The Futurist, January/ February 1988, 45.

[81]Jim Bartimo, "Terrorism Vexing International DP Crime Experts," ComputerWorld, 12 July 1982, 11.

"Computer technology has attracted the ire of terrorists. For example, members of Italy's Red Brigade have bombed computers at a government nuclear facility and research center near Rome; terrorists in West Germany have sabotaged those of private corporations. The computer has come to represent for the politically alienated in many Third World countries the domination of Western civilization. It has become an outlet for their frustrations. The kidnappings and assassinations of business and political officials is giving way to hatred of the machine; few shed tears when computers are attacked. The economical and political losses, however, can be profound; the attackers understand this very well. The computer, by its very mystique, has become a symbol of all the evils we associate with technology."[82]

Through the use of computers, the possibility exists that terrorist groups could be financed through the manipulation and transfer of large sums of money. No longer would there be bank robbers photographed by the bank's cameras, or a kidnap victim to worry about, or even something as simple as fingerprints. The money would simply be electronically diverted into other accounts and withdrawn. One of the best examples was the fraud pulled off in South Korea in the early 1970s.

Through manipulation of a United States Army supply computing program largely operated by Korean technicians, huge quantities of food, uniforms, vehicles, gasoline, and other American supplies were diverted into the hands of a Korean

---

[82]August Bequai, Techno-Crimes: The Computerization of Crime and Terrorism, (Lexington, MA: Lexington Books, 1987).

gang for resale on the black market. The swindle was so effective that the theft of about $18 million worth of equipment a year was being concealed by the misuse of inventory-and-supply computer programs.[83] It is easy to believe that profits from such actions could fall into the hands of organizations not sympathetic to the Security Administrator's own causes.

Although terrorists still kidnap and rob banks for their financial needs, the principal danger to Electronic Funds Transfer Systems (EFTSs) by terrorists is the destruction of wealth and entire economies in an attempt to achieve certain political goals. This is not science fiction. Terrorists indeed pose a threat to EFTSs. Professional terrorists are presently active internationally. Unlike the criminal, the terrorist is activated by ideological fervor. Monetary considerations play a secondary role in the terrorist's activities; what makes the terrorist potentially dangerous is a willingness to sacrifice both himself/herself and others for the cause. EFTSs have already attracted the attention of such groups in France, Italy, and other industrialized nations. Open societies pose a special problem for law enforcement; lax security makes them ideal targets for the politically malcontent. The terrorist thus poses a twofold challenge to the cashless society: a threat to the security of its economic institutions, and a threat to its political well-being. The terrorist has both the requisite weaponry and the will to severely damage key EFTS facilities, bringing a nation's financial institutions to their knees. Of greater concern to society, however, should be the terrorist's ability to force the governing authorities to impose dragonian (sic) measures on their citizens so as to curtail the terrorist's activities. A technologically

---

[83]Thomas Whiteside, Computer Capers, (New York: A Mentor Book, The New American Library, 1978), 37.

advanced society--and one that comes to rely on EFTS for its everyday financial transactions--would find it difficult to preserve its democratic safeguards if its major financial institutions were seriously threatened. The objective of the terrorist is to cause societal havoc, to disrupt a society's political mechanisms. EFTSs are potentially ideally suited for this task.[84]

The 1983 movie WarGames was an amusing but disturbing glimpse into the world of the computer hacker and the computer and telecommunications network that has become increasingly critical to our way of life. In the movie, a teen-aged hacker nearly starts World War III when he breaks into the computer system at the North American Air Defense Command (NORAD) in Colorado Springs, CO. Thinking he had hacked his way into a game, he sends a message to the computer that the computer mistakes for a Soviet missile launch. It was widely publicized that the military had taken precautions to see that this particular scenario could never occur. However, it is a little known fact that the movie was loosely based on Steven Phoades and Kevin Mitnick, teen-aged hackers who claim to have broken into NORAD in 1979. They claim that they did not interfere with any defense operations. Rhoades said "We just got in, looked around, and got out."[85]

Most commercial teleprocessing systems are not nearly as well protected as NORAD. Prominent examples are, as previously mentioned, the EFT networks that links banks and other financial institutions--the four major networks alone carry the equivalent of the federal budget every two to four hours.

---

[84]August Bequai, How To Prevent Computer Crimes: A Guide for Managers, (New York: John Wiley & Sons, 1983), 274.

[85]John Johnson, "'Dark Side' Hacker Seens as 'Electronic Terrorist'," Los Angeles Times, 8 January 1989, 1.

These almost incomprehensible sums of money are processed solely between the memories of computers, using communication systems that are seriously vulnerable to physical disruption and technical tampering. The potential for massive computer fraud or theft is self-evident, but even more worrisome is the danger of a deliberate effort to disrupt the U.S. financial structure. The most serious vulnerability of U.S. banks may not be bad loans to Latin American nations, but rather a way of conducting business over networks that these institutions and their investors now take for granted.[86]

An economy is based on an electronic money system and when ownership of property is based on electronic records rather than on physical possession, the use of computers and data communications invites a different and most effective kind of war. If enough key computers, data communication facilities, and computerized record management centers were destroyed, it would not be any stretch of the imagination to see a society thrown into a deep economic depression and far more easily dominated by the philosophies of terrorist groups.

Access to many systems will present few difficulties to the terrorist. But what is he likely to do once 'inside'? The possibilities are, in fact, considerable. The nationalist/separatist group might access the local police or military computer and extract the names of spies and infiltrators, whom they could then target or feed false information. The group requiring certain materials--explosives, radio-control equipment, etc.--might access the order facility of a supplier's computer and arrange for

---

[86]Richard H. Wilcox and Patrick J. Garrity, eds., America's Hidden Vulnerability: Crisis Management in a Society of Networks, (Washington, D.C.: The Center for Strategic and International Studies, Georgetown University, October 1984), 5.

items to be delivered to a location in which an ambush or hijack can be made. The establishment of a fictitious company is also a possibility, and this might be done with a view to ordering and paying for items electronically which would otherwise be beyond the group's reach. Bacteria samples, for example, are available on the open market but only to bona fide companies or research or teaching establishments. Few, if any, of these suppliers will check to see if a computer-placed order is from a company which has been around for a year or a week. And very often the whole process of ordering, shipping, and invoicing is done automatically by computer. Another possibility is to access intelligence-agency databases and remove the names of wanted persons or to alter important details pertaining to those persons. False and misleading information about politicians or military personnel may be added to a database. When the database is next accessed by operatives, the false data will be accepted as valid and generate serious resource wastage as surveillance and investigative projects are established to confirm or refute implications drawn from the information. Many such intelligence databases are shared by different governments. A computer in Berlin, for example, may be simply accessed by police agents in New York by a telephone.[87]

Terrorists have also discovered another type of computer destruction. Besides physical destruction, militant activists, hackers, and terrorists have been trained to produce logical damage to a computer and its data. The most popular method of causing logical damage is through a crash program which can erase large amounts of data within a short period of time. Known as "Trojan Horses," these computer programs are

---

[87]Michael Conner, Terrorism: Its Goals, Its Targets, Its Methods, The Solution, (Bolder, CO: Paladin Press, 1987).

slipped into existing programs and lie there dormant until someone runs that particular program. Crash programs can be executed at a later date, after the perpetrator has left the company grounds. Through modems, the crash program can even be transmitted to the computer electronically by a phone call from anywhere in the world.

Those crash programs which are executed at a later date are appropriately called "time bombs." The most dangerous modification of these "time bombs" is called the virus program. The first appearance of these were in the United States in 1983. Since 1985 these virus programs have been described in detail in European underground newspapers and hacker information sheets.[88]

Virus programs are self-reproducing programs which copy and implement themselves into other programs and data files to which they have access, spreading through all files, utility programs, operating systems and shared resources of the computer system. This is extremely dangerous, because virus programs carrying damaging instructions can bring down a system in very little time. By the time you have discovered the problem, you may be able to find most of the virus programs and destroy them. But even if you miss one hidden in some forgotten file, that one virus program will begin the problem all over. Now imagine that the virus program contained another program which methodically erased commands, transferred funds, dropped decimal points, etc. You get the picture. The ability to produce logical damage to computer systems, to

---

[88]Ulrich Seiber, The International Handbook on Computer Crime: Computer-related Economic Crime and the Infringements of Privacy (New York: John Wiley & Sons, 1986), 16. Seiber's own footnote on this mention of underground publications states: "See, for example, Die Bayerische Hackerpost, April 1983, pp. 1 et seq."

electronically transfer funds or materials, to crash a system at any time, or to cause statistical and accounting programs to arrive at wrong numbers or conclusions will become the new 'modus operandi' of the terrorist. "Sadly, these viruses and other forms of computer-based terrorism are symptoms of our information age that are likely to endure."[89]

Technologies of destruction, originally aimed toward people and hardware, are turning to another vital commodity-- information stored in computers. Computer viruses are among the newest means available to terrorists seeking to cripple the infrastructure of an increasingly information-oriented society. These viruses pose a significant risk to computers in the defense and commercial sectors.[90]

One of the latest computer viruses to receive a great deal of press coverage was the Michelangelo virus. It got its name when researchers noted that the date it was timed to strike, March 6, 1992, was the birthday of the Italian Renaissance artist, born 517 years earlier. D'Arcy Jenish, author of an in-depth article on this particular computer virus called it a "terrorist virus."[91]

The worst virus yet has recently been released into the computer community. An unclassified Priority Alert message was recently released to all members of the Department of Defense. It read, in part:

---

[89]Mary Culnan, "Electronic Terrorism: How Can We Fight It?" The Atlanta Journal and Constitution, (13 April 1989).

[90]James W. Rawles, "The Viral Threat," Defense Electronics, February 1990, 62.

[91]D'Arcy Jenish, "A Terrorist Virus: Michelangelo Stirs Fears of Future Shocks," MacLean's, March 16, 1992, 48.

"A new type of self-modifying ultra-stealth viruses, called polymorphic viruses, have begun to propagate through the world's computer community. The polymorphic virus scrambles itself using a random number generated by the system clock. By altering every byte of itself when it enters a new environment based on a random number, the newly propagated virus is able to escape detection by most virus scanning programs. The small kernel of code used to unscramble the body of the virus avoids being 'fingerprinted' by interspersing DO-NOTHING statements among those that do the unscrambling (e.g., MOVE A TO A). As the virus copies itself to a new destination, it randomly selects and distributed DO-NOTHING statements from a self-contained list into its own code.

"The 'Dark Avenger' bulletin board system, which disseminates virus code, has recently published the complete source code for the Dark Avenger mutation engine. The mutation engine is a code kernel that can be attached to an existing or future virus and turn it into a self-encrypting polymorphic virus. The mutation engine uses a meta language-driven algorithm generator that allows it to create completely original encryption algorithms. A varying amount of needless instructions are then inserted into the unique algorithm, resulting in decryption algorithms that range in length from 5 to 200 bytes long."[92]

---

[92]Mike Higgins, "Polymorphic Viruses (Automated Systems Security Incident Support Team (ASSIST) 92-38)," from Defense Data Network (DDN) unclassified message traffic, undated.

Eugene Spafford, a computer scientist and authority on viruses at Purdue University in West Lafayette, Indiana, said "Writing these programs is like dumping cholera in a water supply. I view it as terrorist activity."[93]

As virulent as they are now, new generations or "strains" of computer viruses capable of mutating are feared to be the next phase of malevolent software. Such viruses would be able to literally evolve and circumvent viral immunization and antidote programs and hardware. This is because such programs and hardware are designed to check for specific lines of code or specific attributes of viruses. As the mutating computer virus spreads, these computer-virus programs probably would not be able to detect its presence because it has evolved into a new permutation. Herein lies the potential for information devastation from this destructive technology--the viral threat.[94]

The effective Security Administrator must have a background in computer science, and a definite technical background in programming. The reason becomes clear when Tequila, the latest in polymorphic viruses, is described below. Tequila is a virus common in Europe (it was written in Switzerland) and is just now starting to appear in the United States. The technical maturity of such a complex virus is what makes the role of Security Administrator so important. The complex mutating virus is described below:

> "When the user runs an infected .EXE program, the program installs itself on the partition sector of the hard disk using a stealth technique called tunneling.

---

[93]Eugene Spafford, as quoted by D'Arcy Jenish, "A Terrorist Virus: Michelangelo Stirs Fears of Future Shocks," MacLean's, March 16, 1992, 48.
[94]James W. Rawles, "The Viral Threat," Defense Electronics, February 1990, 67.

In the case of Tequila, it puts the processor into single-step mode, and calls interrupt 13H to reset the disk. However, on every instruction interrupt 1 is called, and Tequila has reprogrammed that to look at the location in memory from which it is being called. When it finds that it is being called from the firmware, it stores that address and switches off the single stepping. Now, Tequila knows the address of the hard disk controller firmware and any program that is supposed to be blocking attempts to write to the hard disk via the interrupts is easily evaded by doing a far call to the firmware. Tequila then installs itself on the partition sector.

"The next time the computer starts up, the partition sector runs before any antivirus software runs and installs the virus into memory. Tequila then 'stealths' the partition so that any antivirus software that examines the partition sees only what was there before Tequila came along.

"Now Tequila can start infecting files. It has a complex code generator in the body of the virus, so that the decryptor/loader of the rest of the code is very variable. There are a few two-byte strings that one can scan for and some one-byte strings. However, some scanners have difficulty detecting all instances of the virus and some scanners set off false alarms on some innocent files.

"The virus adds 2468 bytes to each infected file. With the virus in memory, the growth in file size is concealed from programs that ask DOS for this information. Thus, the virus is quite difficult to spot and easily gets copied onto diskettes and passed on."[95]

Do you still believe that anything like this could never happen to you because you live in America? Well, there are various pamphlets and books circulating which tend to describe in detail how to attack a computer center and do a massive amount of destructive work in a minimum amount of time. One such publication is called ECODEFENSE: A Field Guide to Monkeywrenching, published by Earth First!. Under the section on Computers, the book has some interesting things to say.[96]

The attacks on computer centers in Italy and France described earlier indicate that terrorists understand the vulnerabilities resulting from loss of computer services. Should a Security Administrator prepare to defend his or her computer center from this type of attack? If so, to what length must the Security Administrator go to provide a reasonable assurance of protection? Terrorists do not share the world view of their victims, however rational it may be. For the terrorist, the ends are held to justify the means. It is quite logical, therefore, to ensure that the Security Administrator's computer system is not selected by the terrorist as a means. Terrorism generally requires symbols, and conspicuous computers sites have well appeared to be suitable targets for bombings and other physical destruction. Likewise, what does the Security Administrator need to do to prevent hackers, activists and terrorists from entering his or her computer system electronically? These types of computer center security measures against terrorism is discussed later in this paper.

---

[95]Alan Solomon, "Sneaking Past the Scanners: Stealth Viruses, Part II," Infosecurity News, November/December 1992, 29.
[96]Ecodefense: A Field Guide to Monkeywrenching, (Earth First Publishers, 2nd edition), 213-218.

Computer centers of major corporations are increasingly being seen as targets for terrorist activities, particularly in Europe, where attacks on computer facilities of such companies as Bull, Philips, ICL, Honeywell and Litton Industries were politically motivated.

The reaction to such attacks on computer resources in Europe and elsewhere is a renewed effort to protect the facilities from outside risks and the formulation of comprehensive plans in the event of such an attack. Computer security administrators and terrorism analysts expect the attacks to continue, perhaps in greater numbers as the terrorists have come to realize the importance and vulnerability of corporate databases and data processing centers.

Having analyzed the above terrorist incidents, it appears that terrorism against computer centers will indeed continue or even increase and that terrorists will continue to engage themselves mostly in physical or electronic forms of attack against computer centers which entail little risk to themselves. This includes the fairly simple acts of penetrating computer centers and bombing them. One of the latest bombing incidents comes from Peru. On May 14, 1992, six nearly simultaneous explosions were heard in the San Isidro, Miraflores, and La Victoria neighborhoods in Lima, Peru. At the Government Palace in the Rimac neighborhood, terrorists exploded a 1988 Mitsubishi truck that had been stolen two days before in Huancayo. According to the explosives experts, the car bomb contained 200 to 300 kilograms of dynamite. Four persons were injured, including a policeman who had been working in the computer section. The back wall of the building was totally destroyed and the explosion left debris over a four-block area.[97] Later reports identified the computer section as being located at IBM's Peruvian headquarters building.[98]

This was not the first time that IBM offices in South America had been the victim of terrorist bombings. On October 6, 1969, bombs damaged IBM offices in San Miguel de Tucuman, Argentina. Three years later, on November 9, 1972, a powerful bomb exploded and damaged the same IBM offices. On April 29, 1973, an explosion caused extensive damage to IBM corporate offices in San Salvador, El Salvador.[99]

It also appears that terrorists will also increase their electronic penetrations of computer centers and destroy or steal data since it represents little risk to the terrorist as it is accomplished over the phone lines. The information on phone numbers and how to penetrate computer centers via phone lines, how to penetrate the operating systems such as Unix once you have gained entry into the computer, and how to penetrate the data security software packages usually residing on mainframes (e.g., RACF, ACF2, TOP SECRET, etc.), is available through underground 'hacker' sheets, electronic bulletin boards and terrorist-produced newsletters.

The threat of the "intelligent terrorist" requires the Security Administrator's diligence in knowing the computer center's threats, vulnerabilities and existing and planned

---

[97]"Bomb Explodes Near Government Palace; More Attacks Reported," Foreign Broadcast Information Service (FBIS) message traffic dated 14 May 1992. FBIS source was from the Lima Panamerican Television Network (in Spanish) from a 1200 GMT broadcast on 14 May 1992.

[98]John Lamb and James Etheridge, "DP: The Terror Target," Datamation (February 1, 1986), 44.

[99]International Terrorism: A Chronology, 1968-1974 (Santa Monica, CA: The Rand Corporation, 1975), pages 17, 36 and 42. The report was produced for the Defense Advanced Research Projects Agency (DARPA).

countermeasures. The intelligent terrorist that recognizes the value of a computer center as it relates to the fabric of society has now arrived. While terrorists have been mostly launching isolated bombing and vandalism attacks on computer centers around the world, one must be warned of the threat to computer-based networks and the compromise, rather than the destruction, of data by terrorists. Stealing data surreptitiously may cause greater harm to the computer center than actually destroying the computer center and its data.

In October 1985, Georgetown University's Center for Strategic and International Studies (CSIS), in Washington, D.C., warned of the terrorist threat to computer centers in a report entitled America's Hidden Vulnerabilities. The report concluded that computer systems should be safeguarded against acts of terrorist sabotage intended to disrupt or cripple society. The vulnerability of computers to electronic penetration by hackers has increased concerns that terrorists will be following the same logic but with greater destructiveness.

According to Jay Bloombecker, director of the National Center for Computer Crime Data, sabotage of computers by terrorists is one of the highest potential crimes currently worrying experts in international computer crime. "It strikes me as unlikely that bombs will be the way to sabotage computers. The motivation to use computer knowledge against the establishment is there. Terrorists will find the computer an attractive target. We haven't handled terrorism very well in the past and this won't get any better with the introduction of the computer."[100]

---

[100] Jay Bloombecker, as quoted by Jim Bartimo in "Terrorism Vexing International DP Crime Experts," ComputerWorld, 12 July 1982, 11.

When we think about protecting a high-tech resource such as a computer center, most people have a habit of thinking that the threats to a computer center must also be high-tech. But, in fact, a single terrorist with a bomb can do more damage in the shortest amount of time than any high-tech threat could do. Fire is the major problem within a computer environment. Most fires which break out inside computer centers are due to an electrical short circuit or the buildup of deposits of inflammable dust or waste. One danger to computers comes from the mass of cables which are found beneath the raised flooring because the covering of the cables burn easily. It is usually hard to locate a fire under the raised flooring because of the heavy concentration of smoke coming from the burning cables. Of course, fire may occur from the result of an exploding bomb.

Even the terrorist bombs themselves are becoming more sophisticated. Japanese police have reported evidence that shows the bomb planted in a Canadian jet was composed of a timing device constructed with computer chips. Police are also examining the possibility that the same kind of device was used in the terrorist activity that blew a hole in the side of an Air India jet.

The vulnerability of computers to electronic penetration by hackers has increased concerns that terrorists will be following the same logic but with greater destructiveness. Electronic terrorism is feasible now, and potentially effective against financial institutions, military systems, and research and development labs. The debate over the effectiveness of electronic sabotage has recently escalated with the penetration of computer systems at the Naval Research Labs, U.S. Army in the Pentagon, Lawrence Berkeley Labs, Massachusetts Institute of Technology, Mitre Corporation, Stanford University, the University of Illinois, and others. The majority of the countermeasures mentioned in this paper deal with the electronic terrorist. Countermeasures to prevent physical entry into the computer center have already been pretty much analyzed and written about.

The Italians, sensitive to the destruction of computer centers by the Red Brigades, are now preparing their computer centers against such destruction and compromise. The Italian Metallurgical Workers Union has recently blamed the Red Brigades for equipment sabotage at the Italtel plant that makes Protel public switching systems. SIP, Italy's National Telecommunications carrier, has decided to invest 3.2 trillion Lira in a five-year plan that will emphasize data switching and networks with back-up data sites within the Italian computer center community.

Computers themselves are now being used to counter the terrorists. The most advertised counter-terrorist computer is located in Weisbaden, Germany. It is nicknamed "The Komissar." It is controlled by the Federal Criminal Investigation Department (BKA) housed in a cluster of glass and concrete buildings on a hilltop in a suburb of Weisbaden. The staff running the computers and performing the analysis increased from 933 in 1969 to 3,122 in 1979 and in the same period the annual budget multiplied ten times, from 22 million to 200 million marks (about $80 million). The heart of the system is an index of information called the PIOS: Personen, Institutionen, Objekte, Sachen (Persons, Institutions, Movable and Immovable Objects). It stores every clue: address contact, movement, etc. Every address found in a suspect's possession, every telephone number and the name of every person who writes to him in prison, and information about every object found at the scene of a terrorist attack or in a place where terrorists have been is stored among the computer's ten million data sheets. They include, for example, nearly 200 addresses in London that are in some way, however remotely, connected with West German terrorists.[101]

The computer known as the Octopus at the Langley, Virginia, headquarters of the CIA forms the backbone of the U.S. effort against international terrorism; data from every terrorist movement in the world is fed into the Octopus, along with information detailing the movements and activities of known or suspected terrorists. By assembling and digesting myriad bits and pieces of information, experts ultimately seek to predict terrorist behavior.[102]

The FBI's National Center for the Analysis of Violent Crime (NCAVC) is developing a threat model for evaluating proposals for combating terrorist attacks on computer systems. This model uses a threat evaluation model developed from research by the U.S. Army.[103]   The FBI presented this model during a 1989 Defense Advanced Research Projects Agency (DARPA) workshop on responses to computer security incidents.[104]

The Reagan administration became very aware of such potential for electronic terrorism. The administration initiated a new policy requiring federal agencies to identify sensitive information stored in government computers. The new policy reflects the administration's view that data communications and

---

[101]Christopher Dobson and Ronald Payne, Counterattack: The West's Battle Against the Terrorists. (New York: Facts on File, Inc., 1982), 103.
    [102]Neil C. Livingstone, The War Against Terrorism. (Lexington, MA: Lexington Books, 1982), 161.
    [103]U.S. Army, Countering Terrorism on U.S. Army Installations. Technical Circular (TC) 19-16, April 1983.
    [104]David J. Icove, "Modeling the Threat," a committee report presented to the Department of Defense Invitational Workshop on Computer Security Incident Response, Carnegie-Mellon University Software Engineering Institute, Pittsburgh, PA, July 31-August 1, 1989.

government computers must have additional security protection both from foreign adversaries as well as domestic terrorists.

If there were little to worry about on the terrorist threat, then why has terrorism generated such a market for access control systems? A research firm estimated that the access control systems market reached $394 million during 1986 and estimated that the market will grow to $1.64 billion by 1990. Access control systems vendors have increased from 60 to 130 companies in the United States alone within the past few years.

Section 2: Hackers and Hostile Intelligence Agents as Computer Terrorists.

> *"Frankly, we consider all viruses outside of research laboratories to be instances of terrorism."*[105]

One concern that tends to creep into discussions with computer security analysts and security administrators is the possibility that the intelligent terrorist or terrorist group will emerge with a vengeance and wreak havoc on government and commercial systems throughout the world. The dominant threat to the United States is not thermonuclear war, but the information war, where foreign countries are seeking our scientific and economic data.[106]

It is impossible to build systems that are guaranteed to be invulnerable to a high-grade threat; that is, a dedicated and resourceful adversary capable of and motivated to organize an attack as an industrial rather than an individual or small-group

---

[105]Philip Fites, Peter Johnston and Martin Kratz, The Computer Virus Crisis, (New York: Van Nostrand Reinhold, 1989), 51.
[106]Joan M. Hosinski, "U.S. Said to Be Vulnerable in Information War," Government Computer News, 7 August 1989, 41.

enterprise. Such activities have historically been conducted by the intelligence-gathering activities of governments and have generally posed a threat to the confidentiality of information. The rapidly decreasing cost of computer resources, the increased spread of computer technology, and the increased value of information-based assets make it likely that high-grade threats will be encountered from other sources and with aims other than traditional espionage.[107]

The security administrator's worst nightmare is that terrorists of the future may acquire the skills necessary to attack highly sophisticated military and highly-sensitive commercial computer systems. Research discovered a few who believe they have yet to acquire such skills.

Victor Santoro, in his book Disruptive Terrorism, states that "Terroristic attacks on computers are mainly theoretical, as few have yet happened, but there is enough crime by computer on the record to show that it's possible and even likely."[108]

Brian Jenkins, senior managing director of Kroll Associates, has studied terrorism for more than 25 years while in positions with the U.S. government, the Rand Corporation, and Kroll. Jenkins says that thus far, terrorists have attacked computer systems only with bombs, not with advanced hacking techniques. "While it is possible that, in the future, terrorists will

---

[107]David D. Clark, chairman, Computers at Risk: Safe Computing in the Information Age (Washington, D.C.: National Academy Press, 1991), 283. Mr. Clark was chairman of the System Security Study Committee, Computer Science and Telecommunications Board, Commission on Physical Sciences, Mathematics and Applications, National Research Council.

[108]Victor Santoro, Disruptive Terrorism, (Port Townsend, WA: Loompanics Unlimited, 1984), 95.

be innovative enough to hire those with high-tech skills to create havoc, I really don't think that this is their type of crime."[109]

The curious hacker who subscribes to hacker magazines and enjoys cruising through telephone numbers to find the whine of a modem frequency is not what this research paper is about. Neither is it about those who succeed in breaking into computer systems to leave messages of triumph. The hacker discussed in this paper should be considered an external threat, a terrorist, a person who destroys information for spite, revenge, some get-rich-quick scheme, or some ideological reason--but always with physical or electronic destruction or modification of data as a possible end result. These people could be called intelligent terrorists. While it takes little intelligence to throw a Molotov cocktail into a room full of mainframes or even to necessarily gain access to that part of the building, it does take some knowledge of computers and telecommunications to get around automated security obstacles. So, it is curious that Victor Santoro and Brian Jenkins failed to recall the sale of sensitive data to the KGB gleaned from computer systems by hackers in 1986.

Reports surfaced in 1986 of a mysterious break-in through a telephone link at the Lawrence Berkeley Laboratory in California. A 75 cent discrepancy in the accounting summary for on-line charges indicated access to the system by an unauthorized user--a breach in security. Through the persistence of Dr. Clifford Stoll, a system administrator employed at Berkeley, an FBI inquiry was launched in late 1986. Stoll had also been contacted earlier by a systems administrator at the National Security Agency because of several

---

[109]Brian Jenkins, "Defending Your Data," Government Executive, October 1991, 40.

unsuccessful attempts, by a user on the Berkeley system, to enter the NSA computer. Since the intruders had not attempted to destroy files and had attacked exclusively military, nuclear, and defense contractor sites, it was evident that this was some type of espionage operation. After weeks of painstaking tracing and monitoring of attempts to penetrate at least 200 other systems, Stoll, working with system administrators at other sites, eventually followed the hacker's path to Europe.

The criminal investigation carrier out by U.S. and German authorities resulted in the identification and arrest of three West German computer hackers in Hamburg in March 1989. For a full account of this case read Stoll's book.[110]

Information of note published after the book's release included this Reuters newswire report: "West German computer hackers Markus Hess and Dirk Brzezinski and their contact man Peter Carl were found guilty of espionage and given suspended sentences of between 14 months and two years by West German court in Celle. The trio gained access to sensitive information in databases in the United States, Europe and Far East and sold the information to the KGB for $54,000. The KGB reportedly ignored their offer to teach the KGB to gain unauthorized access to databases in return for $600,000. Fourth individual arrested killed himself prior to the trial. The four were discovered by a U.S. programmer investigating unknown charge for computer time."[111] Actually, there was no need for the KGB to pay the hackers $600,000 for learning how to hack the computer networks. They had others working for them as well.

---

[110]Clifford Stoll, The Cuckoo's Egg: Tracking a Spy Through a Maze of Computer Espionage, (New York: Doubleday, 1989).
        [111]"Counter-intelligence Hilite," Reuters Newswire, 17 February 1990.

According to various West German media reports, a KGB espionage ring consisting of computer hackers was neutralized on March 2, 1989 by West German authorities. Press reports indicate that as many as five individuals may have been apprehended. Three of the suspects were arrested in Hannover and were alleged to have penetrated several Western data centers including the Pentagon and a number of hi-tech research laboratories in Japan, West Germany and the U.S. Among the U.S. databases that were alleged to have been penetrated were the Department of Defense's general databank known as Optimus, a NASA computer, and computers tied to nuclear weapons and energy research. The hackers allegedly were providing thousands of computer codes, passwords and programs directly to the KGB with little time delay.[112]

At the time of their arrest, authorities announced that the trio had received several thousand dollars from KGB for diskettes containing sensitive data from databases at the Pentagon, Los Alamos National Laboratory, and NASA. Penetration of several other computer databases in Western Europe was suspected.[113]

An interesting discussion as to whether the U.S. government's computer technology is vulnerable to Libyan or Soviet disruption can be read in Computer Crime Digest.[114]

In a separate incident, it was reported that a West German hacker by the name of Mathias Speer, a computer student who operated from Hanover, West Germany, accessed some rather sensitive databases. According to a Pentagon official [who

---

[112]"Counter-intelligence Hilite," Reuters Newswire, 10 March 1989.
[113]Dr. Lynn F. Fischer, "The Threat to Automated Systems," Security Awareness Bulletin, Department of Defense Security Institute, Richmond, VA, September 1991, 5.
[114]"International Terrorists May Become Responsible For Losses Due To Computer Crimes," Computer Crime Digest, January 1986, 10.

declined to be named], the electronic intruder gained access to the computer database at the U.S. Navy's Naval Coastal Systems Command in Panama City, Florida, and the Air Force Systems Command in El Segundo, California, where sensitive information about U.S. military and intelligence capabilities could have been obtained before the intruder was detected. "We know this was the work of a sophisticated hacker. So you can imagine what a sophisticated signals intelligence service, like the KGB, is capable of doing--not only our unclassified systems, but our classified computers as well," the official said.[115]

Another senior Pentagon official said the collection of unclassified technological data in the United States was a top priority of the Soviet KGB; in some cases unclassified data was more important to Soviet spies than classified material.[116]

A recently declassified U.S. Intelligence Community report on Soviet intelligence collection activities documents the intense efforts of KGB and GRU operatives to acquire high technology related to microelectronics, advanced computer systems, and computer-integrated design and manufacturing.[117] The report reveals that Soviet intelligence collection activities have been aided by on-line access to commercial electronic databases which, although unclassified, contain Department of Defense and government-funded contractor studies dealing with the design, evaluation and testing of U.S. aerospace and weapon systems. The report concludes that in recent years the growing

---

[115]Bill Gertz, "Hackers' Success Worries Pentagon," Washington Times, 19 April 1988, 6.

[116]Thomas David, "Pentagon's Loss of Computer Control Opens Access to Data for Soviets," New York City Tribune, 22 January 1988, 1.

[117]Defense Security Institute editors, Soviet Acquisition of Militarily Significant Western Technology: An Update, (Washington, D.C.: Defense Security Institute), September 1985.

use of electronic databases accessible by remote terminals has provided the Soviets with an efficient means of identifying and procuring unclassified technical information needed by Soviet weapons designers.

Dr. Robert Brotzman, former Director of the National Computer Center, believes that these databases are too inviting for terrorists and hostile intelligence to ignore: "Considering how much fun the bad guys could have on U.S. computers, if they ain't having at them, they're a lot dumber than we think they are."[118] Likewise, this comment: "If the most sensitive computer networks in the nation are vulnerable to teen-age hackers, what could determined terrorists do?"[119] And this reminder from Chuck Cole, deputy computer security manager at Lawrence Livermore National Laboratory: "The whole notion of people breaking into computer systems has been focused on the young college or high school student. That image has to change, because there are some very real dangers."[120] Eric Corley, editor of a national hacker newsletter, 2600, said "It's like a fantasy of being a terrorist without the blood."[121]

NASA was attacked again in September 1987 by a group of West German computer hackers who actually rummaged freely among the data for at least three months before they were discovered. "The West German television program 'Panorama'

---

[118]Robert Brotzman, as quoted by Dr. Lynn F. Fischer, "The Threat to Automated Systems," Security Awareness Bulletin, Department of Defense Security Institute, Richmond, VA, September 1991, 5.

[119]Scott Bennett, "Viewpoints: The Growth of Terrorism," Dallas Morning News, 11 January 1990, 19A.

[120]John Markoff, quoting Chuck Cole, "Top Secret and Vulnerable: 'Unguarded Doors' in U.S. Computers Disturb Experts," New York Times, 25 April 1988, A79.

[121]Mr. Eric Corley, phone interview by author, from Fairfax, Virginia, October 1977.

reported today that once the hackers gained access, they managed to open files labeled 'Shuttle-C study contracts," "system security study" and "booster rocket incidents." Panorama showed 200 printouts it said the hackers had made from the NASA computers."[122]

One of the most alarming penetrations of defense computer systems occurred in 1987 when a 17-year-old Chicago hacker, Herbert Zinn, who went by the alias Shadow Hawk, was brought to trial for the unauthorized theft of software files from Bell Laboratories, the U.S. Missile Command Center, and Robbins Air Force Base. He is reported to have illegally copied software valued at more than $1.2M including complex programs on artificial intelligence and computer design regarded by the U.S. government as "highly sensitive."[123]   Zinn actually went to the extent of placing his break-in methods on electronic bulletin boards and encouraging others to try the same thing. Although claiming he did this for educational purposes, Zinn, the first hacker convicted under the Computer Fraud and Abuse Act of 1986, received a $10,000 fine and a 9-month jail sentence. Installations that Zinn broke in to included AT&T and the North Atlantic Treaty Organization (NATO).[124]

In a democratic society, the right to free speech is tantamount. James Martin stated in 1973 that "there are several organizations with the stated objective of doing harm to computers. One of the organizations is the International Society

---

[122]Serge Schmemann, "Computer Buffs Tapped NASA Files," The New York Times, September 16, 1987.

[123]Dr. Lynn F. Fischer, "The Threat to Automated Systems," Security Awareness Bulletin, Department of Defense Security Institute, Richmond, VA, September 1991, 5.

[124]Ralph Roberts and Pamela Kane, Computer Security, (Greensboro, NC: Compute! Books, 1989).

for the Abolition of Data-Processing Machines, which claims to have several thousand members. It publishes a Manifesto, as do other societies. The actions they recommend mostly fall into the category of nuisance or minor loss, rather than catastrophe."[125] That was 1973. A closer review of computer information more recently published and available in the United States reveals information that borders on the subversive. For example, if one wanted to break into a Univac computer running the Exec III operating system, just read Appendix 3 of Thomas Whiteside's Computer Capers, where the weaknesses of the Exec III operating system is written out in detail. Or read Out of the Inner Circle: A Hacker's Guide to Computer Security by Bill "The Cracker" Landreth. (Microsoft Press, Bellevue, WA. 1985.). Chapter 13 in Ralf Burger's Computer Viruses: A High-Tech Disease, begins with a caveat: "The following program listings involve destructive programs or programs which can be misused for destructive purposes. The main purpose of these destructive programs is to illustrate the weak points in a computer system."[126] The book Covert Surveillance and Electronic Penetration by William B. Moran (Loompanics Unlimited Press, Port Townsend, WA 98368) has a section on how to intercept computer data.

If the Security Administrator is not yet convinced that there are books available in the United States on the subject of computer terrorism, obtain a copy of The Computer Underground: Computer Hacking, Crashing, Pirating and Phreaking by M. Harry (Loompanics Unlimited Press, Port Townsend, WA 98368). This 257-page book describes how to

---

[125] James Martin, Security, Accuracy and Privacy in Computer Systems, (New York: Prentice Hall, Inc, 1973), 323.
[126] Ralf Burger, Computer Viruses: A High-Tech Disease, (Grand Rapids, MI: Abacus, 1988), 225.

defeat computer security, how to pirate software, how to successfully hack your way into Tymnet, Telenet, ARPANET and other bulletin board systems, and how to hack your way past Unix, COSMOS, RSTS, DEC computers, Data General computers and HP2000 computers. Included in this book are sample software programs specifically written for the hacker. One such program is called AutoHacker, a hacking program for use with the Hayes Smartmodem 1200. It automatically dials phone numbers for you and stores the numbers that have a modem whine on the other end of the line in a text file for your later perusal.

The weakness in any computer crime is the pay-off. The criminal has to collect his profit. A terrorist has an easier task. His purpose, unless he's using his computer skills to steal funds or weapons for his group, is purely destructive. From a remote location, he can insert a command to alter or erase records, and be long gone before anyone even notifies the authorities.[127] A terrorist need not even be present at the location of the computer to commit his crime: "A central computer data bank in the United States can be penetrated by a terrorist in the Middle East who simply has access to a telephone line or a computer terminal and the necessary codes."[128] And in another report, a similar stance: "One of the major problems we face in computer security is that, unlike electronic theft or embezzlement, computer espionage is practically impossible to detect. The theft can be conducted remotely by an enemy agent at some random location, such as a pay-telephone booth, without the risk of being physically apprehended. There is no physical evidence

---

[127]Victor Santoro, Disruptive Terrorism, (Port Townsend, WA: Loompanics Unlimited, 1984), 97.
[128]Neil C. Livingstone, The War Against Terrorism. (Lexington, MA: Lexington Books, 1982), 141.

left behind, such as fingerprints or blood types, to incriminate them there."[129]

According to U.S. officials, a group of computer hackers in the Netherlands obtained a large amount of "unclassified but sensitive" high technology data about the Pentagon's Strategic Defense Initiative program. Investigators also suspect that the group passed some of the information to the Soviet KGB intelligence service, which has targeted U.S. computer research networks for years.[130] Government Computer News reported that the hackers had access to crucial information regarding military personnel, the type and quantity of equipment being moved, and the development of important weapon systems."[131] In another article on the same subject: "Teenaged Dutch hackers gained access to computer systems at 34 Defense Department sites during Operation Desert Shield/Desert Storm. They were snooping in sensitive rather than classified military information, apparently through one of the 5,000 worldwide computer networks that comprise INTERNET. Most users are academic and government researchers. The hackers changed software to permit future access, modified and copied military information and even stored some at U.S. universities. A Senate subcommittee criticized lack of progress made since the adoption of the Computer Security Act of 1987 and questioned the vulnerability of other computer systems such as the FAA's air traffic control."[132] As an aside, the possibility of tampering

---

[129] "Real or Imagined? The Hostile Intelligence Threat to Computer Systems," Security Awareness Bulletin, Defense Investigative Service/Defense Security Institute, June 1986.

[130] "Hackers Steal SDI Information," Washington Times, 24 December 1990, 3.

[131] Government Computer News, 25 November 1991, 1.

[132] "Washington Roundup," Aviation Week & Space Technology, 25 November 1991, 29.

with computers critical to air traffic control has already occurred. Six air traffic controllers at New York's Kennedy Airport are suspected of having tampered with a computer that caused a Soviet Aeroflot Ilyushin-62 jetliner, on a trip between Washington, D.C., and New York in January 1980, to travel through airspace reserved for other aircraft. The plane was carrying Soviet diplomats, including the Soviet ambassador to the United States, Anatoli Dobrynin. Letters and numbers indicating the aircraft's radar blip had been removed from the main computer at Kennedy International Airport; thus, the plane's existence in the crowded eastern flight corridor went unnoticed, which could have produced a midair collision.[133] An Aviation Week & Space Technology article states that "More technically adept terrorists could sabotage aircraft by disabling air traffic control computers, either by physically destroying them, inputting incorrect information or introducing computer viruses."[134]

FBI intelligence chief W. Douglas Gow said in a recent interview that the agency has set up a special section to investigate computer-related crime and espionage. Hackers and spies who steal unclassified technology by computer pose new legal difficulties for FBI investigators. Mr. Gow said "they do get sensitive information" that could be used against U.S. national security interests.[135]

---

[133]Neil C. Livingstone, The War Against Terrorism. (Lexington, MA: Lexington Books, 1982), 87.

[134]Breck W. Henderson, "Experts Say Total Security Program Needed to Counter Terrorist Threat," Aviation Week & Space Technology, November 20, 1989, 67.

[135]"Washington Roundup," Aviation Week & Space Technology, 25 November 1991, 29.

A recent General Accounting Office (GAO) report to Congress was highly critical of present federal safeguards applying to computers, maintaining that existing programs are "fragmented and usually did not extend to protect all sensitive data."[136]

In November 1991, two men, a 21-year old student and a 25-year old software engineer, broke through security passwords into the Bronto computer system at Amsterdam's Free University and from there left a trail of destruction across a worldwide university computer network. Once they had broken through, they then keyed into linked university computers in the United States, Spain, Norway, and Italy, changing records and undermining security systems to make subsequent entry easier. A police spokesperson said that damage to the Amsterdam system alone has been estimated at more than 100,000 guilders (US $55,000). They are the first hackers caught by a special unit set up in the Netherlands. They were arrested in late January 1992 and will be charged with fraud, criminal damage and forgery.[137]

Section 3: Computer Resources Being Used By Terrorists.

The newest entry in the field of intelligent terrorism analysis concerns the most recent findings that terrorists from various countries are themselves using computers and automated systems. What we have here are the first indications that the term "intelligent terrorist" is becoming true. However, this field is so new that little has been reported by the public media. There

---

[136]Automated Systems Security--Federal Agencies Should Strengthen Safeguards Over Personal and Other Sensitive Data, (Washington, D.C.: General Accounting Office, Government Printing Office), 23 January 1979, 12.
[137]"Dutch Computer Hackers Leave Global Trail of Damage," Reuters Newswire, 31 January 1992.

are, however, a few ominous signs that have been reported by the media.

Documentation has been found after intense research on the subject matter on terrorist groups in Columbia and Peru, Libya, the Philippines, Spain, and even the United States.

From Columbia, South America: "The army said Saturday it has captured four leaders of a terrorist gang employed by drug kingpin Pablo Escobar to protect his wife and kill his enemies. The death squad--which called itself "Love for Medellin," also acted as a vigilante morals squad, killing prostitutes and homosexuals in Columbia's second-largest city, a military source said. Military officials also were quoted as saying Saturday that they have made new raids on properties linked to Columbia's No. 2 drug lord, Gonzalo Rodriguez Gacha. They said a computer disk [captured in the raid] showed he owned 374 vehicles, all with telephones."[138]

From the Philippines: "In a deadly cross-fire, well-hidden New People's Army troops (NPA, the armed wing of the outlawed Communist Party of the Philippines) opened fire with automatic weapons, grenade launchers and mortars and ambushed two companies of [Mrs. Aquino's Philippine Army] soldiers from the army's 23rd Infantry Battalion as they walked down a lonely mountain road. The government death toll from the five-hour firefight was the worst in nearly a decade: 42 soldiers dead, 16 wounded and five captured. The NPA admitted to six dead.

"Partially as a result [of the ambush], more than 125 provincial and central NPA commanders have been

---

[138]Associated Press editors, "Army Captures Hit Squad Chiefs in Columbia," Dallas Morning News, 10 September 1989, 11A.

arrested, and detailed computer discs, documents and other intelligence materials have been seized."[139]

From Libya: "Two Libyan intelligence officials have been indicted in connection with the 1988 bombing of Pan Am Flight 103 over Lockerbie, Scotland, which killed 270 people, officials in the United States and Scotland announced today. A computer chip found in the bomb wreckage matched the configuration of electronic components of explosives seized in February 1988 from Libyan agents traveling in Senegal, authorities have said."[140]

From Peru, South America: "Peruvian police discovered an MRTA [Movimento Revolucionario Tupac Amaru, also known as the Tupac Amaru Revolutionary Movement] computer center in the district of San Isidro, Lima."[141] The political objectives of this group include the conduct of "armed propaganda" to destabilize the Peruvian Government, to force the U.S. Government and business activities out of Peru, and to create an image of MRTA as the Peruvian militant group aligned with Marxist international revolutionary movements and proponents. Some of the MRTA membership live in Cuba after fleeing Peru in the 1970s after a Government crackdown on student radicals.[142]

---

[139] Bob Drogin, "Aquino Touts Victory Over Communists But Clashes Raise Doubts That Government Has Beaten Insurgency," The Los Angeles Times, 12 March 1992, 46A.

[140] James Rowley for the Associated Press, "Libyans Indicted in Pan Am Blast; Pair Reportedly Intelligence Officers," Phoenix Gazette, 14 November 1991, A3.

[141] "Regional Guerrilla Activities 17-27 May," Foreign Broadcast Information Service (FBIS) message traffic dated 29 May 1992. FBIS source of information came from a Madrid, Spain, news broadcast in Spanish at 0127 GMT, 26 May 1992.

[142] Terrorist Group Profiles, (Washington, D.C.: Government Printing Office, 1988), 111.

A more detailed report on the uncovering of the terrorist data center was published in a Peruvian newspaper:

> TERRORIST DATA CENTER UNCOVERED--During a raid on a ghost enterprise called Optimiza, Inc., at 190 Las Palmeras Street, Apartment 301, in San Isidro two weeks ago, members of the National Antiterrorist Directorate, DINCOTE, found a list with the names of more than 2,500 national businessmen and some 60 members of the judicial branch, including their personal data, the posts they hold, names of the enterprises they run, addresses, and telephone numbers in the archives of a data center that belongs to the Tupac Amaru Revolutionary Movement, MRTA. During a news conference yesterday, DINCOTE agents disclosed that three individuals have been arrested but no names were given. They also disclosed some of the details of the operation, saying that the data center had five modern microcomputers, two of which operated on the 'modem' system which allows them to supply data from one computer to another by telephone. The terrorists also had a fax machine, a scanner, a printer, and 132 diskettes. DINCOTE learned about this data center through documents seized on 14 April from MRTA's second-in-command Peter David Peabody Cardenas Schulte, aka Alejandro."[143]

From Spain: "Civil [Spanish] Guardsmen raided the San Sebastian Provincial Headquarters of the Union of Basque

---

[143]"Roundup of Terrorist Activities," Foreign Broadcast Information Service (FBIS) message traffic dated 5 June 1992. FBIS source was from the FBIS transmitting site located in Asuncion, Peru. Originator was El Comercio newspaper, published in Spanish in Peru, dated 26 May 1992, page A10.

Patriotic Workers (LABLN, the labor arm of the radical Basque Party Herri Batasuna), seizing various documents and computer disks."[144]

The use of computer resources by terrorists can hit pretty close to home. A 150-nation international police organization has begun to study reports of computer and trade networks among U.S., Canadian and European white-supremist groups, including some based in Texas. "Everyone is concerned about the ease with which terrorists may cross borders and their ability to link up," said Don Lavey, head of anti-terrorism investigations at Interpol headquarters in Lyons, France. "But whatever happens, we must adapt," he told the Houston Chronicle. Mr. Lavey said he has been concerned about computer networks shared by terrorist and other extremist groups, including neo-Nazi and [Ku Klux] Klan groups in the United States.[145]

Even the U.S. military concedes that computer viruses can become a part of our own arsenal.

For example, the U.S. Army is looking for help to develop a killer computer virus. "The Army is soliciting bids from small businesses to determine the feasibility of using computer viruses in warfare. It is willing to pay as much as $550,000 to a company that comes up with a plan for creating the programs-- and figures out how to use military radio systems to introduce them into enemy computers."[146]

---

[144]"Update on Anti-Terrorist Operations in the Basque Country," Foreign Broadcast Information Service (FBIS) message traffic dated 14 May 1992. FBIS source was from material released from the Joint Staff, Washington, D.C.; originator was the American Consulate in Balboa.

[145]"Probe Targets Klan; Tax, Rights Inquiry Includes Skinheads," Dallas Morning News, 2 July 1990, 11A.

[146]Rory J. O'Connor, "Army Searches For New Weapon: Computer Virus," Philadelphia Inquirer, 7 May 1990, 2.

General Carl Stiner, commander of U.S. Special Forces, wants commandos to have computer viruses in order to create chaos in an enemy's communications and electronic weapons. On March 4, 1992, when Senator William Cohen on the Senate Armed Services Committee asked Gen. Stiner if he was involved with developing viruses to wipe out enemy computer memories, Gen. Stiner replied: "Without getting into classified areas, I would like to say I think there is a great potential in those kinds of areas."[147] Terrorist attacks on computer centers in the near future may include "high-tech" weapons that are available now. For example, the exploitation of radiated emissions, HERF guns and EMP-T bombs.

Although some skeptics believe that the exploitation of radiated emissions is extremely difficult, this is not necessarily the case. Wim Van Eck, a Dutch electronics research specialist, concluded in a 1985 research report concerning the detection of electromagnetic fields generated by video display units that "A normal TV receiver made suitable for this purpose will in some cases be able to restore information displayed on a video display unit. This reconstruction may under optimum conditions be feasible from distances up to 1 kilometer [.6 mile]."[148]

A terrorist group may also wish to create havoc by shutting down your computer center. A weapon at their disposal is the High Energy Radio Frequency (HERF) gun. It is simply a transmitter composed of a signal generator, an amplifier, and an antenna. It is simply a "point-and-shoot" type weapon from parts that can be obtained from your local electronics store. With this weapon, a high energy pulse can be sent into your computer

---

[147]"U.S. General Wants Ray Guns for Commandos," Reuters Newswire, 5 May 1992.
[148]W. Van Eck, "Electromagnetic Radiation from Video Display Units: An Eavesdropping Risk," Computers & Security, 1985, 276.

center and it will disrupt anything that is running across your wires, including data. The HERF gun can be used to fire signals from the low-frequency end of the spectrum all the way up to microwaves. If the HERF gun can be made portable--and a briefcase-sized weapon is possible--the terrorists will never be caught. Even on the off chance that the Security Administrator figures out that the errors are not caused by the operating system, or a hardware problem or even a virus, how does one find the source of the problem?   Using direction-finding equipment to locate a moving target is a most difficult task.

If you take the concept of a HERF gun to its maximum limit, you will have built an EMP-T bomb; an ElectroMagnetic Pulse Transformer bomb. In its simplest concept, if you turn up the HERF gun's signal high enough, the radiated field will have a most profound effect on the computer.

If the electrical field is strong enough, the silicon boundaries of the computer memory chips will break down. The computer's memory will have been permanently erased as will the data on the hard drives, the floppy disks, and the backup tapes (if you store them in the same area which most centers do). A van is large enough to house the equipment needed to generate such a field. And again, the equipment is available from electronic stores.[149]

Intelligence analysts have warned that if a terrorist group were to construct or otherwise obtain an EMP generator, they could do devastating damage. EMP waveforms are capable of destroying microcircuits and injuring magnetic data storage media. Likely terrorist EMP targets are the financial centers such as Wall Street, the City district of London, or the

---

[149]Winn Schwartau, "Seven Weapons for the Well-Armed Computer Terrorist," Information Security Product News, September/October 1991, 39.

Paradeplatz in Zurich. This would cause incalculable damage to computer hardware and software associated with stock and commodities markets, banking, international currency exchanges, and pension funds. Rebuilding computer systems and restoring software databases from paper records would doubtless take many months.[150]

Section 4: Methodology to Reduce the Vulnerability to Your Computer Center.

> "America's increasingly computerized society will become vulnerable to attacks by criminals and high-tech terrorists unless new computer-security precautions are taken, a National Research Committee announced today."[151]

> "Take your ordinary, garden-variety terrorist. Add a tempting, unprotected corporate target that contains one of the organization's most vital strategic assets--a target that, if knocked out, could lead to major disruptions of service or even to corporate bankruptcy. What you've got is a recipe for disaster--the soft underbelly of the information age--and it's time to shake off some of the dangerous complacency that now exists at corporate and governmental computer data centers across America."[152]

---

[150]James W. Rawles, "High-Technology Terrorism," Defense Electronics, January 1990, 74.

[151]"Washington Digest," St. Petersburg Times, 6 December 1990, 8A.

[152]Michael Beadsmoore, "Terrorism in the Information Age: A Recipe for Disaster?" Computerworld, July 7, 1986, 17.

Whether the threat is the bombing of your computer resources by a terrorist or an electronic attack by an intelligent hacker bent on destroying your data, there are countermeasures that can be taken to reduce the threat.

The author feels that the following requirements are the mandatory minimum requirements which should be in place to protect against a physical or electronic terrorist attack.

The author's own Compu-Terror (Computer Terrorism) Evaluation Plan (C-TEP) describes the events, actions, organizational and personnel responsibilities, constraints, and assumptions required to conduct such an evaluation for a computer system environment. The goals of this C-TEP are to assist the Security Administrator in understanding why a C-TEP is needed; to specify management's scope of involvement; to show the contents of the C-TEP in detail and; to describe how a computer security "Tiger Team" would proceed in analyzing, testing, and evaluating the computer center's anti-terrorist countermeasures already in place. Conclusions and recommendations for additional anti-terrorist countermeasures, if any, would be provided in an "after-actions" report at the conclusion of the evaluation.

There are several different methods and procedures concerning the design and implementation of C-TEPs--each of which, in part, are adequate when used for the specific purposes intended by a "Tiger Team." The methods and procedures described in this C-TEP represent an integration of those found in CSC-STD-001-83 "DoD Computer System Evaluation Criteria," and DoD 5200.28-M "Techniques and Procedures for Implementing, Deactivating, Testing and Evaluating Secure ADP Systems" and various FIPS Publications. The underlying premise was to establish a valid C-TEP against the criteria outlined in DoD 5200.28-STD,

"Department of Defense Trusted Computer System Evaluation Criteria" (The Orange Book) at the author's modified C2 level. In addition, NCSC-TG-005, "Trusted Network Interpretation" (The Red Book) was also used at that level.

The intended audiences of this C-TEP are computer center managers, Security Administrators and others within a data processing community who are specifically responsible for ADP resources and/or who have a genuine need-to-know. Although many similarities exist among ADP facilities, the disparities in equipment, operating systems, criticality of functions, types of customers, geographic locations and other factors tend to make each computer center unique. This uniqueness not only precludes the use of one activity's C-TEP for another, but makes each C-TEP unique to the specific computer center it was placed against. Each C-TEP will list all countermeasures in place meant to ward off possible terrorist threats.

C-TEP DEFINED

The author's Compu-Terror (Computer Terrorism) Evaluation Plan (C-TEP) is an examination and analysis of the security features of an ADP system as they have been applied in an operational environment to determine the security posture of the system against a terrorist attack. Prior to preparing a C-TEP, the Security Administrator should perform a risk assessment of his or her computer center in order to weigh the threats and vulnerabilities of the center. This Risk Assessment should include an analysis of existing and planned counter-terrorist countermeasures for dealing with threats to a sensitive processing environment. With the countermeasures identified, the risks would then be weighed, vulnerabilities anticipated and strategies for coping with realized terrorist threats established. The next logical step would be the testing and evaluating of these countermeasures. This is where the Security Administrator would implement the C-TEP. Implementing the C-TEP would include analyzing the possibility of sensitive data inadvertently or deliberately being taken from the computer room (in clear-text form) and other such major ADP security violations. It is the rising vulnerability of society to terrorist sabotage of information systems that is threatening to be a major issue, and controls to protect against this risk are rarely in place.[153] That is the reason this C-TEP should be seriously considered.

REQUIREMENT FOR A C-TEP

The growing dependence during the last 30 years of virtually all large organizational entities on computer resources continues today at an unprecedented rate. Every computer center reflects this dependency within its user community. Included in the growing scope of computer user support is the requirement to provide access to and processing capabilities for "unclassified but sensitive" data.

Computer center managers consider that the computer is a tool for doing work or providing services which, in practical terms, cannot be done without the computer. Reverting to processing and/or providing access to limited amounts of data, due to a successful terrorist attack, is simply not practical and certainly isn't desirable. A significant threat to the continued success of a computer center would be the loss of processing. This C-TEP offers the Security Administrator adequate assurance that the countermeasures planned and in place will provide the required protection to ensure the surety of continued

---

[153]Richard Baskerville, Designing Information Systems Security, (New York: John Wiley & Sons, 1988), 114.

processing capability and the continuance of the computer center's mission.

MANAGEMENT'S ROLE

The key ingredient in a successful C-TEP is support of the plan by both ADP operations management and senior project management. The fact that support by ADP operations management is necessary is apparent--since ADP operations is the primary participant in the evaluation. The requirement for senior project management support, though perhaps not immediately obvious, is also absolutely essential. The primary reason is that everyone within the computer center, including ADP operations, must understand the importance of the C-TEP and receive a mandate to cooperate to the fullest. In summary, the computer center management should:

- Be aware of, understand, and support the C-TEP.
- Direct that all affected elements of the organization cooperate with the execution of the C-TEP--including computer room contractors.
- Direct the periodic comprehensive testing of the C-TEP and revision(s) as necessary.

The overall responsibility for preparing, testing, evaluating and maintaining the C-TEP belongs to the Security Administrator.

DISRUPTION OF SERVICE CAUSED BY C-TEP IMPLEMENTATION

The "Tiger Team" will implement, test and evaluate the computer center's terrorist countermeasures during normal working hours and, if necessary, after hours and weekends. Testing of certain countermeasures should occur more than once to ensure knowledge of countermeasures across the board by main computer room and site personnel.

Simulating "A loss of power to the IBM 3083 while processing sensitive data" should not occur while demand for the mainframe is high; rather, this simulation should occur during "slack" hours. However, testing personnel procedures should be done during working hours when additional personnel are working.

Items covered in detail later in this C-TEP include consideration of the hardware, software, data, environmental, managerial, sensitive processing procedures, and human resources countermeasures.

Many functions now thought of as belonging to ADP security have traditionally been categorized as a part of good management. A C-TEP evaluation of terrorist countermeasures at an overseas computer center is certainly one of these--as prudent managers have always been aware of the nature of sensitive data and what could happen to them and others if the data were compromised. Unfortunately, however, the ever-increasing growth of sensitive material being processed on computers has not been matched by a corresponding growth in awareness of the need to preserve the sensitive data. Actions and events occurring today, including the penetration of computer systems by hackers, make it increasingly important to recognize sensitive processing for what it is, i.e., a vital element of the organization needing support. In recognition of the importance of sensitive data processing and the need to provide a secure environment, this C-TEP was created as part of the author's ongoing counter-terrorism program.

C-TEP DEVELOPMENT

Two activities are essential for the implementation of an adequate, cost-effective and workable C-TEP. First, the functions supported by the computer center which are critical to processing must be identified. Second, the resources essential to the accomplishment of these specific functions must also be identified. Both should be accomplished by performance of a Risk Assessment and the assignment of countermeasures. This done, the C-TEP can begin in a logical and systematic manner--determining the critical elements to be included in the C-TEP and determining their interrelationships.

CRITICAL ELEMENTS OF THE C-TEP

It is difficult to categorize any one section of the C-TEP as being more important than another. Essentially, each section of the C-TEP is critical and has to be accomplished with equal diligence for the program to be successful. Essentially the C-TEP follows the criteria established in the Orange Book at the C2 level, with some additional criteria at the B1 level included and additional criteria outside the scope of the Orange Book also included. Specifically, the C-TEP tracks with the Orange Book at the C2 level on the following items:

- AUDIT. Must be able to create, maintain, and protect from modification or unauthorized access or destruction an audit trail of accesses into the computer system.
- DESIGN DOCUMENTATION. Documentation must exist that provides a description of the philosophy of protection and how this philosophy is translated into the computer system.

- SECURITY FEATURES USER'S GUIDE. Documentation must exist which describes the protections in place and guidelines on using the computer system.
- SECURITY TESTING. Testing will be performed to assure that there are no obvious ways for an unauthorized user to bypass or defeat the current protection mechanisms.
- DISCRETIONARY ACCESS CONTROLS. Must allow users on the computer system (through default or explicit user action) to protect their files, etc., from unauthorized access from other computer system users.
- IDENTIFICATION AND AUTHENTICATION. The computer system must require users to identify themselves before being able to perform any actions (passwords, etc.). In addition, the computer system must be able to uniquely identify each individual user (USERID).
- OBJECT REUSE. All authorizations in accessing a specific file are negated once the user with those authorizations leaves the file. The next user accessing the same file can only access it based on his or her specific authorizations.
- SYSTEM ARCHITECTURE. Computer system resources must be protected so that they can be subjected to access control and auditing requirements.
- SYSTEM INTEGRITY. Hardware and/or software must be provided to periodically validate the correct operations of the computer system.
- TEST DOCUMENTATION. A document needs to be provided that describes the test plan, test procedures, and results of the testing.
- TRUSTED FACILITY MANUAL. A manual must be provided which shall be addressed to the Security

Administrator about functions and accesses which should be controlled by him or her.

The following are additional items not required at the C2 level but are, nonetheless, required for additional protection:

- Trusted Distribution
- Trusted Facility Management
- Trusted Path
- Trusted Recovery
- Mandatory Access Control
- Labels
- Device Labels
- Label Integrity
- Subject Sensitivity Labels
- Labeling Human-Readable Output
- Exportation of Labeled Information
- Exportation to Multilevel Devices
- Exportation to Single-level Devices
- Design Specification and Verification
- Covert Channel Analysis
- Configuration Management

Of those above items originally required, all exist within the Orange Book at higher levels, such as the B1 level. The five most important items will be discussed in this paper. They are:

- Labels
- Label Integrity
- Labeling Human-Readable Output
- Exportation of labeled Information
- Configuration Management

Many items are also included which did not exist within the constraints of the Orange Book, yet were necessary inclusions to the C-TEP. Those items are:

- DISASTER RECOVERY PLAN. Documentation needs to be evaluated which provides for recovery from various scenarios (fire, water flooding, electrical outages, system crashes, etc.). Documentation also addresses availability of back-up facilities.

- DISASTER RECOVERY TEST AND EVALUATION. Procedures in place to respond to emergencies need to be evaluated, with later testing resulting in fine-tuning the existing procedures. Back-up site should also be evaluated and later tested.

- CERTIFICATION. Someone in authority needs to certify that the computer system meets all applicable Federal policies, regulations, and standards, and that the results of the security testing demonstrates that the installed security safeguards are adequate for the applications (in response to OMB Circular A-130).

- PERIODIC REVIEWS AND RECERTIFICATION. Security is an on-going function. Audits and security tests and evaluations need to be continuously conducted at the computer site.

- MICROCOMPUTER SECURITY. Security at the micro level needs to be evaluated as more and more terminals with internal hard drives reside on those desks which also access sensitive data.

- SECURITY AWARENESS AND TRAINING. A security awareness program needs to be evaluated in response to the Computer Security Act of 1987 for all having access to computer system--management, operations, programmers, users.

PRELIMINARY PLANNING: TEST REQUIREMENTS

Implementation of the C-TEP will require that the system and all its countermeasures be challenged (tested) to determine if the system and its countermeasures react properly to various terrorist actions (e.g., bombing, fire, unscheduled loss of power). Expected results of these tests are usually included in C-TEPs. The procedures that the computer room, other sites, and associated personnel use must also be tested and challenged--without, in some cases, the knowledge of site personnel.

- Scope. The C-TEP as defined and detailed in this research paper will apply to a site encompassing a mainframe, peripheral ADPE inside the main computer room, microcomputers outside the main computer room but attached to the mainframe, the storage areas holding media or material affecting the use of ADPE inside the computer room, the areas and offices around and above the computer room (there will be no offices, crawl spaces or other open areas beneath the computer room) and the personnel who operate the mainframe and/or are involved in handling sensitive media before, during, and after processing. The C-TEP will be structured to accomplish three distinct security activities:

  o Determine whether the necessary terrorist countermeasures are in place to counteract the terrorist threat;

  o Test and evaluate these specific countermeasures using a formal methodology;

- o Observe, in an informal manner, any computer security improprieties not necessarily covered under specific terrorist countermeasures (e.g., observing someone looking in their wallet or purse for their password).

- Expected Results. It is anticipated that all countermeasures in place will be adequate in reducing the overall risks of operating a sensitive-processing computer room and a remote site operating in an on-line mode. It is also expected that any terrorist countermeasures which still need to be put in place will be minor in nature and will not affect the data processing (e.g., the posting by the nearest telephone of Department of Defense (DoD) instructions on "How to Handle a Bomb Threat").

- Methods Used. Individual test methodologies are listed by their areas of consideration and by specific countermeasures in "Preparatory Actions" of this C-TEP.

- Assumptions. The major assumptions, which will affect the outcome of the C-TEP, concern the availability of key personnel to participate in the conduct of the C-TEP and the accessibility of the C-TEP team to the computer environment (i.e., the total system). C-TEP Team members will require broad access to the system in order to test and evaluate all of the terrorist countermeasures. This availability of and accessibility to the system will also require availability of key ADP operations personnel for escort, to respond to questions, to react to loss or impairment of countermeasures and to assist in making the C-TEP a smooth flowing and unrestricted operation. It is further assumed that the Security Administrator and appropriate security personnel will spend the required time observing and assisting in the implementation of the C-TEP.

It is also assumed that information derived from the testing and evaluating of terrorist countermeasures will be treated in a sensitive manner--in such a way as to allow for the tracking back of any discovered inadequacies to the responsible individual or procedure. It is assumed that certain personnel-related countermeasures will be tested and evaluated--including active duty military, civil service employees, and contractors involved in the processing, and handling of sensitive data on the computer system.

TEST TEAM

This section should describe the "Tiger Team"--its members and their responsibilities, their access capabilities, special permissions, limitations, and, testing and evaluation strategies.

- <u>Team Members.</u> For this hypothetical C-TEP, a "Tiger Team" would test and evaluate the terrorist countermeasures in place, assuring that sensitive data is securely processed in an interactive on-line mode. Rather than relying on individual efforts, this team should remain together and assist one another in implementing each formal countermeasure scenario. Informal observations will be individually made and recorded and later reviewed by the team for inclusion into the C-TEP Report. The team should be identified at this point.

  The combined experience of the team should cover the entire realm of terrorist countermeasures being tested and evaluated for this particular C-TEP. Any additional assistance, outside that of the Security Administrator, and participating ADP operations personnel, would be nonproductive.

- Special Permissions. The C-TEP team should test and evaluate countermeasures (some more than once) over a period of days--including weekend and evening tests of certain countermeasures if necessary. Countermeasure testing should encompass a variety of security areas, including physical and environmental countermeasures, hardware and software countermeasures. As a result, the C-TEP team should accrue an amount of information on the computer center's vulnerabilities not usually gained by individual users, programmers, or possibly even the Security Administrator. Therefore, the responsibility of the "Tiger Team" is to bring management's attention to the entire spectrum of knowledge gained from the implementation of the C-TEP. To successfully accomplish this task, the C-TEP Team needs to be equipped with a blanket "need to know" policy--allowing the C-TEP Team full access to hardware, software, data, etc. This permission needs to be instigated by management and circulated among those staff participating in the C-TEP during normal working hours and during the evening and weekend shifts.

In turn, the C-TEP Team should execute the C-TEP in a timely manner, creating as little disruption as possible to computer center personnel and operations. There is no need for the Security Administrator to be physically present during all testing and evaluating. However, the Security Administrator should be accessible if needed during the testing period. A limitation to be considered is the needed presence of the Security Administrator during evening and weekend countermeasure testing. Access by the C-TEP Team to the system site, or to computer center personnel should not be prevented or denied at any time.

PREPARATORY ACTIONS: TEST METHODOLOGY

The C-TEP is an examination and analysis of the counter-terrorism security features on a computer system, applied in its operational environment. The C-TEP will be the final determining factor upon which accreditation is based.

Basically, the C-TEP Plan is designed to accomplish two major objectives:

- To determine whether the necessary countermeasures, as chosen in the Risk Assessment, have been installed; and,

- To determine whether the installed terrorist countermeasures are working effectively.

A five-step approach will be used to determine the extent to which the objectives are met:

- Identify qualified individuals capable of evaluating and reporting on the installed terrorist countermeasures. [The "Tiger Team" would meet this requirement.]

- Review the Risk Assessment for currency and accuracy, identifying and analyzing the nature of the terrorist threats, computer center vulnerabilities and their respective countermeasures.

- Develop the C-TEP. This plan describes how each countermeasure will be exercised to determine its effectiveness. Since a "Tiger Team" will be attempting to defeat certain system protections, information on these attempts will be found in this plan. Simple scenarios, walk-through inspections, documentation reviews, and procedural reviews will be utilized and will also be found in this plan. This plan will be modified during the actual C-TEP if unanticipated situations arise.

- Execute the C-TEP. Conduct the terrorist countermeasure tests and evaluations indicated in the following paragraphs. Document the C-TEP activities as the implementation proceeds--identifying discrepancies and problem areas, if any, so that recommendations can be made for inclusion in the C-TEP Report to the Security Administrator.

- C-TEP Documentation. This final step documents the results of the C-TEP. This report will include a recommendation to the Security Administrator to accredit or not accredit the system based upon the level of risk identified by the C-TEP team. If non-accreditation is recommended, the C-TEP Report will contain the appropriate recommendations regarding security deficiencies and their resolution.

The fourth step of the five-step approach warrants elaboration of the component areas--discussed by countermeasure area (i.e., software, hardware, administration procedures, physical, environmental, personnel and management) and within each countermeasure area by a detailed listing of how the testing and evaluation will be conducted. The C-TEP methodologies are as follows:

- **AUDIT**

  The Orange Book states that a current computer system should be able to "create, maintain, and protect from modification or unauthorized access or destruction an audit trail of accesses to the objects it protects. The audit data shall be protected by the computer system so that read access to it is limited to those who are authorized for audit data. The computer system shall be able to record the following types of events: use of identification and authentication mechanisms, introduction of objects into a user's address space (e.g., file open, program initiation), deletion of objects, actions taken by computer operators and system administrators and/or system security officers, and other security-relevant events. For each recorded event, the audit record shall identify: date and time of event, user, type of event, and success or failure of the event. For identification and authentication events, the origin of request (e.g., terminal ID) shall be included in the audit record. For events that introduce an object into a user's address space and for object deletion events the audit record shall include the name of the object. The ADP system administrator shall be able to selectively audit the actions of any one or more users based on individual identity."

While the authentication and identification areas addressed in the Orange Book referenced above are better responded to in the section on Identification and Authentication, there are still a number of audit capabilities and audit-related areas which can be addressed in this section. These are addressed as follows:

Residue Control. After completion of any data processing on the computer system, the operating system may allow a portion of the data to remain in some resource sharing storage. This data may then be compromised by electronic terrorists who may succeed in a direct attempt to access your information. Failure to clear memory can contribute to accidental disclosure of the data and could also contribute to the success of probing attempts.

The risk of allowing data to remain in memory or on-line storage is significantly reduced by purging or erasing all resource-sharing accessible storage areas. This purging or erasing must be accomplished before memory and on-line storage device locations are released by the Security Administrator or system operator. Software areas may be purged or erased by either a software program or a hardware clear switch.

Password Protection from Visual Observation. Log-on attempts, unique passwords and the authentication process was evaluated for the hypothetical system and is detailed in later sections of this book. This accountability of protecting your own password includes those cleared users inside the computer sites, especially the system operator. If a password of an authorized user of the sensitive processing system is displayed on the terminal screen or on hardcopy, the password may be compromised.

To prevent this, the C-TEP team should check that the current sensitive processing system is providing some mechanism to protect passwords from being displayed on the terminal screen or on any printouts observed. For those that are displaying the password on the monitor screen or on hard-copy printouts, software is available that will either suppress printing of the password when entered or present a strikeover field on which the terminal operator can enter a password. Such mechanism should be in place for sensitive processing.

Tape Storage and Data Encryption. The sensitive tapes being run should be physically removed from the computer site and secured after the processing period. Floppy disks containing sensitive data should also be secured in an appropriate manner. Because of the newest threats of HERF guns and EMP-T bombs, it is wise to keep your tapes in another area of the building or even off-site.

While various levels of protection may exist for different, but sensitive, media (e.g., Privacy Act, AGENCY SENSITIVE, FOR OFFICIAL USE ONLY, etc.), these sensitive data files could be encrypted to reduce the possibility of compromise through disclosure. Encryption provides a terrorist countermeasure which protects the files as off-line media. However, this protection provides no protection while files are being processed as clear text. Responsibility within the sensitive processing system for the removal of sensitive tapes from the computer room and assuring adequate security should belong to the Security Administrator.

Inspections of Software. Software may have intentionally placed "trap doors," or may be retaining access availability known only to the person or vendor who created or supplied the software or to former computer room operators. To conduct periodic inspections of the sensitive processing site's software, the C-TEP team should implement one or more of the following:

o Make visual inspections of program listings and files to detect unusual instances of data or software differences.

○ Perform automated code matches. A program can be developed to compare files for exact matches. These files can contain software or data.

○ Verify the current date or modification level identifier of the configuration item which is assigned whenever a file is modified. Compare this date or identifier against the approved configuration item date or identifier (e.g., when the file was modified for authorized purposes). This requires that the system be able to maintain the last date of access to a file or maintain configuration management procedures used to control the application programs.

○ Compute and securely store checksums for software and data files. Then, periodically checksum each file and compare the result to the stored checksum. A checksum is computed based on a portion of the data in each record.

Changes to mission-specific software (systems and application programs) should be under software configuration control, employing recognized software configuration management procedures and software identification techniques. To be effective against maliciously or accidentally entered faults, such checks and the governing software algorithm may normally be stored under restricted access conditions. As applied against error accident, the check and its algorithm serve best when continuously accessible by the system and employed as part of the diagnostic process.

Controlled Use of Assembly Language Coding.
Assembly language software provides the most direct access to hardware and software features that may be

manipulated. The C-TEP team should check each of the following alternatives to see which can effectively minimize the risk of penetration to the operating system:

o Physically remove the assembler language processor from the sensitive processing system.

o Control access to the assembler language processor through the use of passwords. Limit the issuance of these special passwords to those programmers who have a valid requirement to use assembler language.

o Place the assembler language processor on an off-line storage medium so that it cannot be used without the active cooperation of the computer console operators or the site security officer who will have to mount the off-line storage medium to the computer.

Terrorists may choose to attack a computer center by planting malicious "bugs," resembling programming errors, in computer software, thereby making computers malfunction. "Like mines in naval warfare, all software warfare bugs are carefully designed to be small and hidden and leave few telltale traces, even after being activated with devastating effects, such as causing repeated crashes of a major computer system."[154]

Security Editing and Accounting. Deficient input and output procedures may damage the integrity of operational files. This could result in decisions being made based on invalid and inaccurate data. The C-TEP team should check that strong edit and transaction

---

[154]Scott A. Boorman and Paul R. Levitt, "Deadly Bugs," Chicago Tribune, May 3, 1987, 19.

accounting features are in place to ensure data integrity. Some controls that the Security Administrator should have are:

o Controls on input, such as transaction counts, batch totals, and machine-readable document input. Types of input validation checks include:

- Character checks such as testing for numeric, alphabetic, or specific character groups, blanks, field separators or special characters, and the proper or valid arithmetic sign;

- Field checks such as testing for limits, ranges, valid item, consistency, and sequence.

o Controls on processing, such as transaction counts, batch control totals, validation by file reference, consistency checks, and control on rounding errors.

o Controls on output, such as item counts, control totals, trailer labels on data sets, control records, or serial numbers on documents (e.g., social security numeric). Example of an input/output control group's typical responsibilities include the following:

- Log in jobs received for processing from user departments.
- Check document counts and control totals of work received.
- Notify user department that the work has been received and indicate whether the counts and totals are correct.
- Note any work that was due but not received.
- Note and initiate action on any improper preparation by the user departments, such as failure to provide counts or totals.

    – Submit documents to be entered.

EDP Auditor. To prevent inadequacy of system controls, the Security Administrator should acquire professional EDP audit expertise. Considering the growth of typical computer centers, a full-time internal ADP audit specialist should be available to carry out EDP audits of the system. With an EDP auditor, the Security Administrator should feel that management can be assured about the adequacy of counter-terrorist security and can be notified on a timely basis of any realized threats or additional weaknesses on the system.

Requirements and Participation of an EDP Auditor. EDP auditors, along with the Security Administrator, should participate in the development of security requirements for important applications systems to ensure that the security requirements are adequate and that adequate controls have been specified. A list of certified EDP auditors is available from the Association of EDP Auditors; these auditors are required to sign off on all formalized application system requirements and specifications. The auditability and security of application systems is strengthened and can reduce the cost of both internal and external security audits.

    The C-TEP team should recommend that the Security Administrator periodically review EDP auditor participation and ensure that all significant application systems receive audit attention.

Computer User Trouble Call Logging. All calls from users and staff regarding problems with a computer and communications system should be logged detailing the caller's name, the time and date, and the nature of the problem. A brief disposition report should then be prepared for each problem report.

The C-TEP team should recommend that the Security Administrator should be able to review each of the problem disposition reports to determine that a problem was satisfactorily resolved and also to determine that there were no adverse impacts of the solutions provided (e.g., a correction of the operating system may have some side effect with a security or privacy implication). This practice forces user and staff liaison people to justify their actions and to document each correctional action that they have taken. The log can then be analyzed by performance monitoring and by the EDP auditor and/or software or system development people for possible improvements of the current operating environment.

Independent Control of Audit Tools. Audit programs, documentation, and test materials need to be kept in secure areas by the site security officer; Audit programs should not remain in the data center tape library. The audit programs should not be kept on disk or in any other way kept on the system where they might be subject to tampering.

Computer Systems Activity Records. Most computer systems produce a number of auditable system activity logs, journals, and exception reports. Such recordings should be periodically and selectively examined both manually and through automated means by the site security officer, looking for key indications of possible unauthorized activities. Such recordings on tape, disk, and sometimes paper listings should be archived for a reasonable period of time and records should be kept to ensure that no reports are missing. For example, printed console logs should be on continuous forms. Any breaks in the forms should require signatures indicating integrity of operation and no missing pages. In one computer installation the console logs should be examined on a sample basis monthly. All logs should be dated and timed with an indication of operational personnel on duty at the time the logs were produced. It may be necessary to keep manually written logs of some computer operation activities, especially at some overseas sites, to compare with or complete the automatic logging of system activity.

The C-TEP team should evaluate such records and see if they are adequate.

Employee Identification on Work Products. All computer operators and other employees should have standard identification in the form of official names, numbers, and/or passwords. This identification is to be entered into all records, data input, and activity logs and journals to identify workers associated with all work products. Identification can be accomplished by manual signatures or keying of identification into equipment keyboards. Data entry clerks should be required to initial all batch control forms used for data entry and enter identification into computer input data. Computer operators should sign computer console printer listings or enter their codes through console keyboards indicating the starting and ending of work periods. Print-outs should also have the requestor's name or identification on the cover sheet.

- **DESIGN DOCUMENTATION**

The Orange Book states "documentation shall be available that provides a description of the manufacturer's philosophy and an explanation of how this philosophy is translated into the computer system. If the computer system is composed of distinct modules, the interfaces between these modules shall be described."

This design documentation is formally called the Network Security Architecture and Design report. The Network Security Architecture section of the report must address the security-relevant policies, objectives, and protocols. The Network Security Design portion of the report must specify the interfaces and services that must be incorporated into the network so that it can be evaluated as a trusted entity.

- **SECURITY FEATURES USER'S GUIDE**

    The Orange Book states that "a single summary, chapter, or manual in user documentation shall describe the protection mechanisms provided by the computer system, guidelines on their use, and how they interact with one another."

    This user's guide needs to be prepared which describes user visible protection mechanisms at the global (networked) level and at the user interface level of each component (and the interaction between them).

- **SECURITY TESTING**

    The Orange Book states that "the security mechanisms of the ADP system shall be tested and found to work as claimed in the system documentation. Testing shall be done to assure that there are no obvious ways for an unauthorized user to bypass or otherwise defeat the security protection mechanisms of the computer system. Testing shall also include a search for obvious flaws that would allow violation of resource isolation, or that would permit unauthorized access to the audit or authentication data.

Back-up Personnel Control. The loss of one person whose corporate knowledge of the system is lost with him, such as the loss of the Security Administrator, should have minimal impact on the continuing operation of the sensitive processing system. Such persons should have an assistant working with him or her at all times so that the loss of the person primarily responsible, whether planned or unplanned, would allow the assistant to step in and continue operating.

Testing and Debugging. The procedures for testing and debugging software may be inadequate. If there is a software failure during sensitive program testing or debugging, it may be difficult to determine the state of the computer and ensure the integrity of data that was on-line or otherwise readily accessible. In the period of system instability during a software failure, normal system safeguards may not be in effect.

The C-TEP team should suggest that the Security Administrator look at two programs: one system program and one application program. The Security Administrator should ensure that the testing and debugging of both programs are done during the appropriate time in a controlled environment. Specifically, in systems software, the testing and debugging should be performed initially during dedicated time in a controlled environment. If operational user files are required for testing, copies of these files should be used. Operational testing may be carried out when quality assurance personnel are satisfied that the programs are operating reliably.

In application programs, the testing and debugging may be permitted during nondedicated times, but, again, only copies of data files should be used.

- **DISCRETIONARY ACCESS CONTROLS**

The Orange Book states that the "computer system shall define and control access between named users and named objects (e.g., files and programs) in the ADP system. The enforcement mechanism (e.g., self/group/public controls, access control lists) shall allow users to specify and control sharing of those objects by named individuals, or defined groups of individuals, or by both, and shall provide controls to limit propagation of access rights. The discretionary access control mechanisms shall, either by explicit user action or by default, provide that objects are protected from unauthorized access. These access controls shall be capable of including or excluding access to the granularity of a single user. Access permission to an object by users not already possessing access permission shall only be assigned by authorized users."

Password File Encryption. The file access control mechanism in the operating system may not prevent a skilled penetrator or "hacker" from obtaining the on-line password file. This may lead to a further penetration of the computer system and the disclosure of sensitive or sensitive information. Also, the data security software package may not be able to encrypt data.

The C-TEP team should suggest that a password encryption algorithm be employed, resulting in storage of passwords in encrypted form only. Alternately, the file containing the passwords used to log-on to the system can be encrypted. Such a scheme will prevent an on-line password file from being readily intelligible if the file is disclosed. The password file is stored in encrypted form using a one-way or irreversible algorithm. The encrypted passwords cannot be inverted to obtain the original clear text passwords. In operation, user supplied passwords are encrypted and compared against the encrypted passwords in the file. A match indicates that a valid password was supplied. Presumable, if a hacker or terrorist is able to gain access to this file, then the other access control authentication mechanisms could also be bypassed. Encrypting the password file is an effective measure against disclosure and casual browsing.

Clearances/Identification of Personnel. All sensitive processing system users should be cleared to the level of data classification they are allowed to access. Although an individual may be cleared to CORPORATE SENSITIVE, the individual user should also have a need-to-know to be established by management.

The C-TEP team should verify the existence of up-to-date clearances of those involved with sensitive data processing, including contractor personnel. The C-TEP team should also verify the procedures used in gathering and storing such information. For example, since all Federal Government employees undergo a National Agency Check (NAC) up to and including SECRET on them before being hired, it is recommended that managers be aware of what those background checks revealed before allowing recent hires access to sensitive data on the system. The ability to pass a NAC may not be a clear indication that the person should still be allowed onto the system; access should be permitted on a case-by-case basis by management only after careful inspection of the investigation.

Participation of Personnel During Sensitive Processing. System users, including those providing input data and using output reports, should supply explicit control requirements to systems analysts and programmers who are designing and developing application systems. Users should also be required to explicitly agree that necessary controls have been implemented and continue to function during production use of the sensitive processing system and programming maintenance.

Users' understanding of their own applications is enhanced significantly when control specifications are required from them. Users are placed in a position where they can make better decisions regarding the appropriate controls in some aspects of applications and determine recovery time requirements. Users become knowledgeable of and sensitive to the needs for computer security and privacy. Sharing of responsibility of accountability for control is enhanced. Separation of duties is also enhanced. Completeness and consistency of controls is facilitated.

Library Access Control. Computer program libraries containing listings of programs under development and in production and associated documentation should be protected from unauthorized access. In large organizations, a full-time or part-time librarian may be used to control access, logging in and logging out all documents. The program library should be physically separated by barriers from other activities. Documents should be distributed only to authorized users. It may be necessary to enforce strict access control to programmers' offices as a means of protecting programs and documentation. Programmers should have lockable file cabinets in which they can store materials currently in use. A clean desk policy at the end of each working day may be justified as an extreme measure. Program and documentation control is particularly important when using or developing licensed software packages because of the strict contractual limitations and liabilities.

This demonstrates the importance of computer program assets to the organization. It provides separation of duty among programmers to ensure that programmers have access only to the documentation and programs within their areas of responsibility.

- **IDENTIFICATION AND AUTHENTICATION**

The Orange Book states that the "computer system shall require users to identify themselves to it before beginning to perform any other actions that the computer system is expected to mediate. Furthermore, the computer system shall use a protected mechanism (e.g., passwords) to authenticate the user's identity. The computer system shall protect authentication data so that it cannot be accessed by any unauthorized user. The computer system shall be able to enforce individual accountability by providing the capability to uniquely identify each individual ADP system user. The computer system shall also provide the capability of associating this identity with all auditable actions taken by that individual."

Separation and Accountability of ADP Functions.
Holding managers accountable for the security in the

areas they manage requires that these areas be clearly and explicitly defined so that there is no overlap or gaps in the managerial control of ADP functions. ADP functions should be broken down into as many discrete self-contained activities as is practical and cost-effective. Besides being a good general management principle to maintain high performance, identifying specific functions also provides the necessary explicit structure for assignment of controls, responsibility for them, accountability and a means of measuring the completeness and consistency of adequately meeting all vulnerabilities. Separate, well-defined ADP functions also facilitate the separation of duties among managers, as is required in separation of duties of employees. This reduces the level of trust needed for each manager. The functions of authorization, custody of assets, and accountability should be separated to the extent possible.

Separation reduces the possibility of accidental or intentional acts resulting in losses. More efficient ADP functions are created and the possible loss of control is inhibited from migrating from one function to another. However, increased complexity of ADP functions could result from excessive separation of functions, making the application of individual controls more difficult.

Terminal User's Agreement. A terminal user should be required to read and comply with a list of items initially brought up on the terminal screen when the user first enters the system. Upon transfer, the user is also required to read and comply with the terms ending his use on the system. It is recommended, for at least legal implications, that these forms be created and signed as appropriate. It is not enough to give employees handling sensitive data a packet of DO's and DONT's; a legally binding form where they agree not to divulge sensitive data, etc., should be incorporated.

Employees are the weakest link in computer security-- little if anything stops them from walking in and out of their computer center with floppy disks, modems, printouts, etc., except warning them that they had better not get caught.

Terminal Identification. The Security Administrator's computer system may have improper or insufficient authentication of hardware. This can lead to a situation where the operating system cannot properly identify a terminal before responding to a request for data. There is then the possibility that data will be rerouted to a terminal whose location is not secure enough to support the display or storage of the data.

Each remote terminal should be individually identified by a hardware feature in synchronization with the operating system. That is, the communications port should always communicate with the same terminal unless physically switched by an authorized person.

- **OBJECT REUSE**

The Orange Book states that "all authorizations to the information contained within a storage object shall be revoked prior to initial assignment, allocation or reallocation to a subject from the computer system's pool of unused storage objects. No information, including encrypted representations of information, produced by a prior subject's actions is to be available to any subject that obtains access to an object that has been released back to the system."

The C-TEP team should find this to be true. Allowing someone to continue processing from a terminal in which someone else failed to log-off may result in the next user observing data the new user may not have seen under their own log-on user identification (userid) and password. Employees traditionally tend to walk away from their terminals and leave them on--this would allow anyone else from using that terminal, with the consequence that if anything went wrong, the person who had previously logged in would get blamed for it.

- **SYSTEM ARCHITECTURE**

  The Orange Book states that "the computer system shall maintain a domain for its own executions that protects it from external interference or tampering (e.g., by modification of its code or data structures). Resources controlled by the computer system may be a defined subset of the subjects and objects in the ADP system. The computer system shall isolate the resources to be protected so that they are subject to the access control and auditing requirements."

  Redundant Equipment. In some situations even short periods of downtime due to equipment failure may pose a serious threat of denial of service if there is no back-up hardware or contingency plan.

  While the criticality of operating the current sensitive processing system is fairly low at this time (uptime requirements only), it is anticipated that as the number of terminal sites increase and the amount of sensitive data increases, the reliance, and thus the criticality of uptime requirements, will also increase.

Enough redundant equipment should be available from vendors, contractors, and support organizations to carry on the minimum critical functions in the event of an equipment failure in the main configuration.

Concerning tape back-ups, in many sites daily or weekly back-ups are kept in the same room as the computer equipment--they should be kept in the same building but not in the same room. It is also true that secondary back-ups are often kept off-site at an employee's home--notwithstanding the allegiance of the employee, they should be kept in a more secure place.

Concerning back-up sites, there should be one. If a computer center goes up in flames because of a terrorist attack or is destroyed by a natural disaster, the computer center loses its ability to process data. No commercial back-up company may be capable of handling the current configuration; many computer centers have one-of-a-kind equipment, equipment so old that they are not even held in vendor warehouses anymore, and special communication configurations. These configurations make these sites so unique that no matter how much money is thrown at the problem after the site is destroyed, a computer center could not be up and running for many months.

Interruption Resistant Power. The power supply for the sensitive processing system may be inadequate to meet the facility's future performance requirements. The C-TEP team should evaluate various solutions to ensure that there is no weakness. For example, the C-TEP team should inspect these items:

- o The installation of a voltage regulator transformer to correct for minor power line fluctuations (transients). This regulator will provide protection against minor transients and brownouts.
- o The use of a motor alternator with an energy storage flywheel to protect against short-term power failure.
- o The use of batteries to protect against long-term power failures.
- o The use of a back-up generator to supply electricity to the system during a graceful shutdown.

Access to Sensitive Processing Computer Sites. The physical aspects of the computer facility may make it difficult, in some ways, to control access to the facility.

Appropriate physical security controls, employed to safeguard the equipment, apply not only to the computer equipment itself and terminals, but also to such removable items as listings, magnetic tapes, etc. The point is to protect not only the user's data and programs, but other components of the system configuration as well. Since part of the computer system (e.g., magnetic disks, tape files or copies of machine listings) contains sensitive data, it may be necessary to separate them physically and to control access to them independently. This applies to the environmental facilities required to provide reliable operation of the system. One solution is to install an access system to prevent unauthorized persons from entering the ADP facility. The following systems provide protection by requiring the entrant to unlock a door and may be used singly or in combination: conventional key and lock set; electronic key system; mechanical combination locks; and electronic combination locks.

One example seen at various processing sites is the air intakes which draw outside air into the building. These are sometimes at ground level, rather than being on the roof or otherwise protected. The introduction of noxious or caustic agents/fumes at the intakes, such as hydrochloric acid, would cause damage to computers and other equipment. The introduction of carbon monoxide, (e.g., an exhaust pipe of a car next to the air intake), would not be noticed and could injure site personnel. The environmental support system for the computer site buildings should be separate from the environmental support system for the computer room.

The C-TEP team also usually finds that some computer centers plainly advertise themselves as an ADP facility; the C-TEP team would suggest not advertising your buildings as one that holds ADP equipment. The C-TEP team also usually finds that access to many of the computer sites by vehicles is possible right up to the physical building. There are usually no protections to stop that. The C-TEP team would then suggest placing a perimeter fence around the buildings if possible and installing card readers for entry behind the fence. As a minimum, the team would suggest that large concrete planters be placed at the entrances so that vehicles could not run up onto the curb and run through glass doors into the lobby. One computer center had such concrete barriers, but the planters were spaced too far apart to stop a car or even a truck from going between them.

Physical Layout. The physical layout inside the main computer room and other sites networked into the mainframe may make it difficult to control the movement of persons within the ADP facility.

The C-TEP team should inspect that procedures exist which minimized access to the computer area on a need-to-know basis. Visitors, cleaning personnel, maintenance personnel, and customer engineers should be required to provide identification, a valid reason for access, and should always be escorted.

Fire Protection. Fire protection may be inadequate, making the processing facility vulnerable to loss or damage by terrorist actions and the resulting fire.

The C-TEP team should look at the following appropriate protections:

o   Installation of a fire/smoke detection system. Place additional fire/smoke detectors above false ceilings, below raised floors, and in air conditioning ducts. Install a control panel that can identify the location of the detector that has identified the fire or smoke. At some computer sites, the C-TEP team can usually find neither smoke detectors nor overhead water sprinkler in the entire building, much less the computer room. The C-TEP team have also found asbestos in the ceiling on every floor, making the cost of putting in an overhead water pipe system for fire suppression very expensive as the asbestos will need to be removed. In case of a fire, the asbestos will keep the firefighters away from the scene, as asbestos-laden smoke is carcinogenic. At one computer site, a C-TEP team found that if someone pulled a fire alarm from anywhere inside the building, someone then also had to manually call the fire department. The alarm should automatically ring at the fire department because people will tend to forget to make that call if there is a real fire. At another computer site, there was no water drain under the raised floor in computer room; probably because there was no overhead water sprinkler installed; however, any water introduced into the room to fight fire would add increased weight to the computer room floor and may buckle it. Worse, the floor could fail. Smoke alarms should also be placed in air return ducts.

o Make fire extinguishers available in accessible locations. Mark each extinguisher as to the type of fire for which it is to be used. For example, Class A extinguishers should only be used on paper, wood, or other material that would leave ashes (unlike electrical or cleaning fluids (fuel) fires).

o Provide a means of extinguishing or controlling a fire in the ADP facility by installing an automatic fire extinguishing system. Three types of such systems are: a water sprinkler system, a carbon dioxide system, and a HALON-1301 deluxe system. Install alarms to alert personnel if the system has been activated. A water flow alarm can be used for sprinkler systems, and a pressure sensor alarm can be used for gaseous systems.

o Provide a fire protection plan to reduce the cause of fire and to extinguish a fire quickly. Develop the fire plan with the aid of the local fire station. Conduct frequent inspections to identify and eliminate potential fire hazards.

o Make plastic sheeting available to cover equipment to protect against water damage. Store magnetic tapes and removable disk packs in fireproof or fire-resistant containers or rooms.

o One needs to also look at the use of Emergency Power Off (EPO) switches in and around the computer rooms. At one computer site, EPO plungers were only located at exits in the rear of the computer room, none at the two main entrances into and out of the computer room. The C-TEP team suggested EPO switches be placed at those exits. At another site, there was no EPO switch in the computer room at all to disable electricity to computers in case of electrical fire. There was no Uninterruptible Power Supply (UPS) at that site, either, so loss of electricity would crash the tape heads. At this particular site, the building's back-up generator kicks in 4-5 seconds after loss of main power, which is too long for the computers to remain running.

Environmental Control System. The environmental support systems (air conditioning, heating, and humidity controls) may be inadequate to meet ever-increasing performance requirements.

The C-TEP team should research and report on at least three appropriate protections:

o Installation of multiple units to protect against the failure of the air handling unit (AHU). For example, use three 20-ton AHUs in place of one 50-ton AHU. There should be enough capacity to maintain the environment with one unit out of service. The AHUs circulate the computer room air, provide temperature and humidity control, and filter the air.

o If the environmental control system fails, the capability to use outside air may be beneficial. Depending on location and weather, the use of direct outside air via vents and fans may be sufficient to maintain the temperature and humidity of the facility.

o Install the AHU designed to use and recirculate inside air in the event that outside air becomes unusable. The outside air may contain high amounts of noxious fumes or may be of such poor quality that the filtration system would not be useful. Even a rumor of toxic germs released in a ventilating system (remember the Legionnaires' disease in Philadelphia) could keep occupants outside of a building for days, shutting down any computer and communication centers inside as effectively as if they had been physically damaged.[155]

The C-TEP team would suggest that the Security Administrator test for the following areas:

o Loss of air conditioning
o Loss of humidity control
o Loss of heating

Discarded Document Destruction. Input/output documents, including any human readable documents or non-erasable computer media, should be reviewed for

---

[155]Richard H. Wilcox and Patrick J. Garrity, eds., America's Hidden Vulnerability: Crisis Management in a Society of Networks, (Washington, D.C.: The Center for Strategic and International Studies, Georgetown University, October 1984), 2.

potential loss sensitivity and appropriately destroyed when no longer needed. Appropriate protection of materials awaiting final disposition should be used. Logging of all actions to ensure an audit trail and adherence to rules is essential. Strict assignments of tasks and accountability are essential. Documents such as obsolete system development materials, test data and manuals should be considered. This provides complete accounting for all documents, reduces exposure to loss in facilities and trash, makes facilities less cluttered, reduces fire hazards and reduces cost of storage.

Physical Security. The physical perimeter within which security is to be maintained and outside of which little or no control is maintained should be clearly established. All vital functions should be identified and included within the security perimeter. Physical access control and prevention of damage immediately outside security perimeters should be carefully considered. For example, physical barriers should extend to the base floor and to the base ceiling around sensitive areas. Areas beneath false floors and above false ceilings should be controlled consistent with the control of working areas between them. Important equipment (such as electrical power switching and communication equipment and circuits) should be made secure and included within the security perimeter. Employees and on-site vendors should be made aware of perimeters on a least-privilege basis. The perimeter should be easily discernible, simple, uncluttered, and sufficiently secure relative to the value of assets inside the perimeter. Drawings and specifications of the perimeter should be available and used for planning any facilities changes. Additional barriers between areas with different security requirements within the exterior barrier also should be established.

Emergency Preparedness. Emergency procedures should be documented and periodically reviewed with occupants of areas requiring emergency action. Adequate automatic fire and water detection and suppression capabilities are assumed to be present. After a physical attack by terrorists, reduction of human injury is the first priority, followed by saving other important assets. Emergency drills that enact the documented procedures should be periodically held. It should be assumed that occupants of an area in which an emergency occurs do not have time to read emergency procedures documents before action. Procedures should include activation of manual alarms and power shutoff switches, evacuation routes, reporting of conditions, safe areas for regrouping, accounting for all occupants, use of equipment such as fire extinguishers to aid safe evacuation, and actions following complete evacuation. A hierarchy of emergency commands should be established with backup assignments. Emergency drills should be organized to minimize loss of critical activities such as computer operation. Close supervision of drills by managers, who are aware of practice drills or real emergencies, is necessary. Large, clearly visible signs, providing basic directions, are required. For example, locations of fire extinguishers, portable lights, and emergency switches should clearly be identified with signs that can be read from the most likely work stations.

Unattended Periods. Many computer rooms are manned at least 8 hours a day. There may occur unforeseen events which cause the computer room to be unmanned for various lengths of time. The computer room and other sensitive sites are sensitive areas which, during unattended times, should be made physically secure with locked doors, significant barriers, and automatic detection devices for movement or natural disaster losses. Periodic inspection by guards is also important. In addition, sensitive areas, not generally visible to others, should never be occupied by a lone employee for reasons of safety and prevention of malicious acts. Adequate control of unattended periods will ensure consistency of security.

Smoking, Eating, Drinking Prohibitions. Smoking, eating, and drinking are not permitted in computer equipment areas. Prevention requires signs, written policy, enforcement, and the rigorous application of penalties. In addition, personal grooming and dress codes should be voluntarily practiced to avoid interference with moving parts of peripheral equipment and personal injury. In addition to obvious benefits, these rules would also prevent the remote chance of a smoke detection or water detection alarm being triggered unnecessarily.

If a C-TEP team encounters evidence of smoking, eating or drinking within a computer room environment, they can be assured that the countermeasures against terrorist actions are also lax.

Traffic Minimization. Access authorization should be granted on a privileged basis. Three access levels can be granted: general, limited, and by exception. General access is granted to those whose work stations are in a restricted area. In one computer room this included computer operators, maintenance staff, and first-level supervisors. Limited access is granted, for specified periods of time, to those responsible for performing specified preplanned assignments, such as auditors, security personnel, and repair or construction crews. Finally, exceptions can be made in emergencies as long as those having access are escorted and, after which, extraordinary measures are taken to ensure integrity of the area. Application programmers no longer need access to computer rooms except on an emergency basis. Systems programmers need access on a limited basis. Visitors would be restricted entirely from computer rooms unless by exception and are accompanied by a high-level manager who explicitly accepts responsibility for the visitor. Other sensitive areas, such as programmers' offices, job set-up areas, and data entry work areas, should be similarly restricted to authorized access. Signs identifying limited access areas should be posted, and rules should be strictly enforced. Also, computer peripheral equipment requiring human operation should be in rooms separate from computer equipment requiring little human attention. Unauthorized physical access is one of the greatest security vulnerabilities and is effectively reduced by careful placement of computing activities.

Alternate Power Supply. A power supply, independent of the original source for uninterrupted service, should be provided by batteries charged from original power--providing a few minutes of independent power or by an independent power source such as a diesel generator for longer durations. An alternative source of energy, such as a diesel generator without batteries but with adequate power quality regulators, can be used when uninterrupted service is not important, but long durations of outage are harmful. This control is needed only where power is sufficiently unreliable relative to the seriousness of computer failure or unavailability. The location, environment control, and access security are important to ensure integrity of the alternative power equipment and fuel. Periodic full tests are important for maintenance.

Materials Storage and Access. Equipment, such as telephone switching panels and cables, utilities, power and air conditioners, computer devices, and supplies (e.g., such as paper, tapes, and disks) should be placed or stored to ensure their protection from damage and to minimize the adverse effects they may have on other items. Dust, vibration, chemical effects, fire hazards, and electrical interference could be introduced into the computer environment by terrorists. Items requiring special safeguards should be isolated to reduce the extent of required safeguard coverage. In multi-floor buildings, vertical as well as horizontal proximity should be considered.

Separation of ADP Equipment. Different types of computer equipment (central processors, disk drives, tape drives, communications equipment, printers, power supplies, tape libraries, terminals, consoles) require different environments for optimum operation and different numbers and types of operations personnel. Therefore, they should be placed in different rooms with appropriate separation walls, distances, and accesses. For example, printers create dust and vibration from paper movement and should be separate from disk and tape drives that are sensitive to air quality and vibration.

Again, if the Security Administrator is allowing these situations to occur, then the countermeasures against terrorist actions are also probably lax.

Magnetic Media Library. A simple physical security survey is usually performed by the C-TEP team on the Magnetic Media Library (MML). Items surveyed include the use of battery operated emergency lighting to facilitate the safe exit of personnel from the library in the event of a power failure; deadbolt locking device to secure the room when it was not occupied; the placement of an automatic door closer so that the door would not remain ajar; two-hour fire ratings of the walls; doors and door frames should be of metal not wood; installation of a smoke/fire detection device, especially in ductwork; and installation of a fire suppression system.

Inspection of Incoming/Outgoing Materials. Certain materials and containers are inspected, and entry or departure is restricted. Within constraints of all applicable laws and personal privacy, any computer operator should prevent movement of materials and inspect contents of closed containers into and out of the computer room. Mail bombs have been delivered to computer centers with devastating results. Materials may include tapes, disks, listings, equipment, recorders, food and beverages, chemicals, and such containers as lunch boxes and briefcases. Unneeded materials should be stored outside for later retrieval by owners. Authorization forms may be used to control movement. Spot checks and posted signs rather than continuous inspection may be sufficient.

Flooding/Water Protection. The C-TEP team would inspect the computer room and other sites for overhead water pipes and inspected the adjacent rooms, including the floor above, for water pipes. If an overhead water sprinkler system existed, the type (reaction or preaction) will be brought to the Security Administrator's attention. If water pipes do exist in or near a sensitive computer, the flooding drill should be tested by the Security Administrator. Restrooms have been bombed by terrorist groups with the resulting flow of water running onto computers and flooding computer centers.

- **SYSTEM INTEGRITY**

     The Orange Book states that "hardware and/or software features shall be provided that can be used to periodically validate the correct operations of the on-line hardware and firmware elements of the computer system."

     Software Engineering Tools. The failure of software to perform according to specified requirements has the potential to compromise security. Software failure may, for example, destroy the integrity of a particular database or allow inventory shortages to go unnoticed.

     The C-TEP team should conduct a preliminary overview of the software engineering tools available to those whose software will be running in the sensitive batch processing mode. These tools aid the development process and provide an increased confidence that software will perform reliably and in accordance with stated requirements. The C-TEP team should look at what currently exists or is being used, including:

     o Research in Secure Operating Systems (RISOS) tools developed to analyze Assembly language programs. Analytical tools available in RISOS include a program that counts occurrences of a specified symbol, a program that identifies the control flow and flags specified items, and a program that locates instruction patterns. These are some of the software engineering tools developed specifically for security.

o Software quality measures are computer programs that examine a program to generate a quantifiable measure of the program's quality. This allows testers to reject programs with quality measures that are outside a certain range, on the assumption that program reliability decreases as quality decreases.

o Self-metric software examines the source code of a computer program and inserts software measurement probes. Data gathered from such probes might indicate the number of times a loop was executed, entry and exit values, and the test stimuli provided. This data helps testers estimate the extent to which a program has been tested.

o Test data generators are computer programs that generate test cases to be used in software testing. These programs range from utility type programs that generate sequences of alphanumeric and/or numeric data based on parametric inputs, to entire systems that interpretively examine the flow through a program and attempt to generate appropriate sequences of test cases.

o Audit programs insure that programs conform to a given set of programming standards. Programs that deviate significantly may be more difficult to understand and may have flaws that could affect security.

- ○ Trace programs record data such as program variables or events that can assist in program debugging and validation.

Suppression of Incomplete and Obsolete Data. The dissemination and use of incomplete and obsolete data should be prevented or restricted. The suppression of incomplete and obsolete data will prevent decisions from being based on such invalid information. This also prevents the privacy of a data subject from being violated. It allows databases to be updated (old and irrelevant information may be deleted), thus reducing operating costs and potentially increasing performance.

The C-TEP team would verbally review dissemination policies and procedures for reasonableness and compliance with regulatory, statutory, and civil requirements; review procedures to block dissemination of certain types of information; and review procedures to expunge records from certain databases. The reviews would be made with Security Administrators who were found to be adequately aware of such compliance and who were also aware that obsolete and incomplete data were handled in the same manner as the more active on-line sensitive data.

Personal Data Inspection. Many computer centers belong to organizations that receive and disseminate data files from and to outside sources. As such, the organization should have an input/output control group. This group checks the data files when they are received and disseminated. It checks for the inclusion of improper data fields, such as individual names and social security numbers. Also, more sophisticated checking of the relational aspects of the data field is done to determine whether individuals can be identified by combining information from multiple fields. The group screens all files to be received and investigates anomalies. A log should be kept of all activity.

In this manner, potentially sensitive, privacy and confidentiality problems are caught early before data are made available to outsiders. This group should also examine data to see that the organization's standards are met with respect to items such as format, content, and value.

Human Subjects Review. Besides handling the sensitive level data, the computer system may also handle Privacy Act data. The manner in which individual privacy (data confidentiality) is handled is a key issue and would be further inspected by the C-TEP team. The C-TEP team should investigate three main areas:

o Sensitivity of system operators to issues of privacy.
o Personal values associated with the handling of Privacy Act Data.
o General competence and ability to cope with unforeseen situations in which Privacy Act data is compromised.

Input Data Validation. Validation of all input to a sensitive processing computer system should be performed in both applications and computer operating systems to assist in the assurance of correct and appropriate data. Validation should include examination for out-of-range values of data, invalid characters in data fields, exceeding upper and lower limits of data volume, and unauthorized or inconsistent control data. Program errors, dependent on the content or meaning of the data, should also be checked.

The C-TEP team would suggest that the Security Administrator review systems design documentation to determine that input data controls are appropriately designed into the system. Run tests, using erroneous data to check on the functioning of validation controls, should also be performed.

Also, if missing essential data are still missing beyond a certain time limit, steps should be taken to obtain the appropriate data. This procedure acts as an error correction/detection control--identifying records for which important information is still missing after a certain period of time (the update could have been misplaced, processed incorrectly, inadvertently omitted, etc.). Such a procedure preserves personal privacy--ensuring that incomplete records, which could cause misleading decisions, are reduced. The control also helps keep records up to date.

Protection State Variables. If the mainframe does not employ two or more protection-state variables, both the user and the operating system should operate in the same state. As a result, a hacker could be able to perform hardware functions without restriction.

The C-TEP team should ensure that the processor has at least two protection-state variables (e.g., privileged mode and user mode), in which certain instructions are illegal except in privileged mode. Examples of privileged instructions include input/output, memory management and context switching. Modification of the protection-state variables should be contained by the operating system and hardware so that a program in user mode cannot switch itself into privileged mode.

Memory Protection Mechanisms. The architecture of the mainframe may not include mechanisms to restrict main memory access by user software programs. Lack of memory protection mechanisms also makes it possible for user software programs to interface either inadvertently or maliciously with other user software or with the operating system itself.

The mainframe should support the use of memory protection mechanisms. These mechanisms are designed to isolate users from each other and from the operating system. The hardware checks each fetch and store instruction for proper access. Examples of hardware protection mechanisms include memory bounds registers (CDC 6000 series), storage locks and keys (IBM 370 series), segmentation (IBM 360/67), paging (HONEYWELL 6180), rings, capabilities, tagged architecture (BURROUGHS B6700), and descriptor-based protection (Plessey 250).

Hardware Error and Tampering Detection. Undetected hardware errors or hardware tampering may compromise security. The C-TEP team should check to see if the mainframe and microcomputers have been provided with facilities to detect and expose internal hardware malfunctions. Modern hardware normally has error detection capabilities, such as parity error detection. Hardware components should cause an interrupt to occur whenever there is a change in their status. Software can then be developed to intercept the interrupt for possible tampering or change in hardware configuration. Software may also be developed to detect unusual error or interrupt patterns.

Data Accountability Assignments to Personnel. Users should be aware and formally assigned the responsibility for the accuracy, safekeeping, and dissemination of the sensitive data they handle. If the data processing department does not handle data properly, then it is up to the users to require corrections. Organizationally, users provide a data processing department with the resources to assist them with their functions. In terms of controls, users should be able to tell data processing what is required in terms of data accuracy, relevance, timeliness, handling procedures, etc.

The C-TEP team realizes that this may run contrary to many current organizational structures where data processing, in some sense, controls the users. However, the team should review organizational assignment of responsibilities for computer security matters; and discuss with both user and data processing management their mutual responsibilities regarding computer security and privacy. The C-TEP team should also review procedures in which users correct records, control the dissemination of records, and otherwise actively participate in the enforcement and design of computer security controls.

Protection of Data Used in System Testing. Application and test programmers usually need test data to develop, debug, and test programs under development. In some cases, small amounts of fictitious test data can be generated independent of users and production data. However, many application programs require significant amounts of test data that are exact copies of a full range of production data. Test data are frequently obtained as samples of entire files of production input data currently being used, or recently used, for the application being replaced or as output from other preprocessing computer programs. There is sometimes significant exposure by providing current production data to programmers. Often data can be obtained from obsolete production input data files, but in some cases even these data may be confidential. Customers for whom production programs are being developed should be made aware of the exposure problem, and should obtain advice and assistance for producing test data in the least confidential but most expedient manner. Sensitive test data should be treated with the same care as equivalent production data. In any case, development and test programmers should not be given access to real production files in a production computer system except in the case of emergency and then under highly controlled conditions.

This control can greatly reduce the exposure of an organization to a wide range of errors, omissions, and intentional acts. It also imposes a beneficial discipline on development and test computer programmers.

Production Program Authorized Version Validation. The authorized versions or copies of production programs, according to identifiers, are checked with a list of authorized copies and changes made to the production programs to determine that the version of a production program to be run is authorized. Update of the list is part of the ordinary maintenance process of production programs. Separate test and production program libraries are maintained.

This prevents unauthorized versions of the production programs from being executed when used in conjunction with other related controls. Accidentally running a test version or an old version of a production program can be prevented and detected using this technique. Unauthorized versions of production programs can be similarly detected and prevented from being run.

The C-TEP team would suggest that the Security Administrator examine, where feasible, the logs showing all exceptions (compile dates that do not match). The Security Administrator should follow up on instances where a match between the list of authorized versions does not match the identifiers.

Computer Programs Change Logs. All changes to computer programs should be logged into a permanent written document. The log can be used as a means of ensuring formal approval of changes. This enables review of the purpose, time, type, and individuals who made changes. This control aids in researching problems that occur; utility programs that maintain program libraries in the computer are useful as they can automatically log change activity.

Exceptions Reporting. Exceptions reporting on a timely basis should be built into the computer operating system, utility programs, and application systems to report on any deviation from normal activity that may indicate errors or unauthorized acts. For example, if a user defines a data file that allows anyone access to it, a message should be printed out warning the user, and possibly the operations staff that the file is not protected. Exceptions reporting should occur when a specific control is violated, or the exception report may constitute a warning of a possible undesirable event. Exceptions reports should be recorded in a recoverable form within the system and when necessary for timely action displayed to the computer operator, or in case of on-line terminal use, displayed to the terminal user.

Technical Review of Operating System Changes. Whenever any change is to be made to the computer operating system programs, a review of the change is made. The intent is to make sure that the new changes are valuable and will not compromise controls and integrity, have an unanticipated impact on some other part of the system, or interfere excessively with vendor updates.

The C-TEP team would suggest that the Security Administrator review the logs of system changes and compare them with the actual changes.

- **EVALUATION DOCUMENTATION**

The Orange Book states that "the system developer shall provide to the evaluators a document that describes the test plan, test procedures that show how the security mechanisms were tested, and results of the security mechanisms' functional testing."

This Security Test documentation should establish a plan to examine, analyze, test and evaluate each protection in place on the system. Each protection is "challenged" to determine if, and how well, it reacts to various adverse conditions. The test documentation reflects the evaluation findings, conclusions and recommendations made by the C-TEP Team.

- **TRUSTED FACILITY MANUAL**

The Orange Book states that "a manual needs to be addressed to the ADP system administrator that shall present cautions about functions and privileges that should be controlled when running a secure facility. The procedures for examining and maintaining the audit files as well as the detailed audit record structure for each type of audit event shall be given."

Security Administrator Functions. Security is a full-time job and the Security Administrator should have adequate authority to manage an appropriate security program.

The position or function of the Security Administrator, including duties and responsibilities, should be established in writing. The Security Administrator should be located within the ADP facility organizational structure so that the Security Administrator reports directly to the appropriate authority on matters concerning security of the sensitive processing system. Functions of the Security Administrator should include:

o Serve as the single point of contact for ADP security at the respective ADP facility.
o Analyze or assist in analyzing the ADP environment and identify weaknesses, assess threats, and apply protections when needed.
o Develop, maintain, and document security requirements and operating procedures.
o Insure that all personnel who install, operate, maintain, or use the ADP system know system security requirements and their responsibilities.
o Establish methods for detecting, reporting, investigating, and resolving ADP security incidents.

o Establish procedures for controlling changes to system hardware, software, applications, passwords and central facility and terminal access.
o Conduct or assist in conducting periodic audits of security procedures and controls.

The C-TEP team should check that the Security Administrator has been granted the appropriate authority and has the appropriate training to carry out the responsibilities.

Software Development Procedures. Software development procedures at the computer facility may be inadequate to insure that software is developed and controlled according to standards.

Management should establish and publish a Configuration Management Plan which describes software development procedures and change procedures and places explicit controls on the development and change processes. The plan should cover the areas of program design, coding, and documentation. Program design should include:

o Audit trails to establish an historical record of processing.
o A thorough and comprehensive plan for program testing.
o Controls on the accuracy of data, such as input verification, matching against legal values, control fields, and self-checking digits.
o Quantitative controls, such as transaction counts, batch control totals, controls on rounding errors, reasonableness checks, and error suspense files.

Program coding should include:

o   Programmers organized in teams, making sure that no single programmer is responsible for an entire sensitive application system.

o   Structured naming conventions so that all references to a data element within an application are called by the same name.

o   Use of comments explaining accompanying code segments. These comments ease the task of program maintenance and help provide documentation.

o   Use of standardized indentation of source code to improve both readability and maintainability.

o   Use of a second programmer/analyst to inspect every program before it is compiled to ensure it conforms to standards, does not use restricted functions, and is logically complete.

Program documentation should be standardized within the computer center and should contain:

o   A functional description of the program written in a narrative form describing the initial definition of the program and any subsequent changes.

o   A program or subprogram section that contains information about the hardware environment, design elements, and interfaces.

o   A program specification section that describes the program inputs, outputs, functions performed, interdependences, and exception conditions.

o   A program manual section with flowcharts, source listings, cross-reference listings, test data used, and operating instructions. These standards may have to be adapted to individual facility needs.

Software Maintenance Procedures. The procedures governing the maintenance of production computer software may have weaknesses that lead to a compromise of security.

Management should establish and publish a Configuration Management Plan which describes the software maintenance procedures that place explicit controls on the maintenance process. Controls on the software maintenance procedures should include:

o An approved "Request for Change" should be required to initiate changes in production programs.
o Program changes should be coded, tested, and documented in accordance with software development and acceptance procedures. These controls may have to be adapted to individual needs.
o New software releases should be advertised in advance and properly identified by version or modification identifiers.

Processing Procedures. The computer center may have inadequate procedures for the acceptance and release of data.

Input/output procedures should be established that place explicit controls on the submission of input and receipt of output. The input/output procedures should:

o Require the system to log job requests when users request a sensitive production run.
o Identify persons authorized to submit and pick up work from the sensitive processing computer facility.
o Control housekeeping activities to maintain the flow of work through the ADP facility.
o Provide all users with instructions for obtaining and returning tapes and disks to the magnetic media library.

○ Provide instructions to cover the signing of receipts upon receiving sensitive material and obtaining a receipt for sensitive output.

Access Procedures. Inadequate procedures for controlling access to the sensitive processing facility or site, media library and supplies area may lead to disclosure, theft, fraud, modification or destruction.

Procedures should be established for controlling access to the sensitive processing facility, supply storage area, and other associated sites such as remote terminal areas and back-up sites.

Methods for controlling access to the ADP facility may include:

○ Access lists
○ Escort procedures
○ Identification badges
○ Guards
○ Mechanical or electronic door locks
○ Prompt removal of transferred or terminated employees from access lists and the mandatory turn-in of any facility identification or access keys or cards.

Periodic inventories should be conducted of computer equipment and related supplies.

Waste Procedures. Existing procedures at the ADP facility may be inadequate for disposal of ADP waste material.

Procedures should be established that clearly define the ADP waste materials that are to be disposed of in a secure manner and that provide the sensitive processing computer room with site(s) for secure disposal. These procedures should identify and provide destruction facilities for:

o Paper and paper products, including carbon paper
o Printer ribbons
o Magnetic tapes, disks, drums, memory, etc.
o Microfilm and microfiche.

Destruction facilities include incinerator, shredders, disintegrators, pulp machines, magnets, and tape degaussers.

Emergency Procedures. Security procedures for emergency situations may be inadequate, absent, or unenforceable at the ADP facility.

Well-conceived and technically feasible emergency procedures should be established and tested periodically. Sources of advice for the development of these procedures include:

o Local fire and police department
o Local National Weather Service
o Buildings and Grounds manager
o Overall ADP security manager

These procedures will normally:

o Provide for off-site storage of duplicate records and files
o Arrange for processing critical applications at other ADP facilities
o Identify materials to be evacuated or destroyed
o Designate a single point of contact for developing emergency procedures

- Provide transportation in the case of emergency evacuation

Operating Procedures. The operating procedures may be inadequate and lead to disclosure, destruction, or modification of data, or a denial of service.

Operating procedures should be established that clearly and explicitly state how the sensitive processing system will function on a day-to-day basis. Some of the points that these procedures should cover include:

- System start-up, shutdown, and system crashes
- Priority scheduling of production runs
- Computer operations personnel interface with users and programmers
- Separation of duties
- Rotation of duties

Personnel Controls. Poor management controls and policy can lead to lapses in security.

The controls listed below provide various solutions depending on the vulnerability:

- To prevent lapses in security, management should actively comply with security regulations and control procedures and make sure that employees do the same. Training and indoctrination courses should be given regularly to employees.

- To prevent misuse or damage to the sensitive processing facility, screen all potential civilian and military employees for personal integrity, stability, and conscientiousness. Maintain close and effective communications with the staff to prevent employee dissatisfaction or to deal with complaints as they rise.

o To improve safety and security, periodically observe the work environment and work habits of employees. Observation will detect poor housekeeping habits that may increase the possibility of physical losses, such as magnetic paper clips or magnetic screwdrivers left near or set on tapes and disks, trash left in computer room, or coffee cups and soft drink cans left in computer rooms. Observation will also detect poor work habits that may compromise security, such as listings left unattended or files left open for unauthorized browsing.

Personnel Compromise. All personnel having system access (e.g., Development Office Staff, users, contractors and visitors) can represent a degree of weakness that could be exploited by hacker or terrorist to compromise security.

To reduce the weakness of a compromise of sensitive information, all personnel with unescorted access to the ADP facility should be required to have a security clearance. The level of clearance should be at least as high as the level of information being processed. Uncleared personnel should be escorted by authorized persons, and sensitive information should be protected.

To reduce the risk of inadvertent damage by personnel, employ competent and well trained personnel. Make clear the duties and obligations of employees.

Assets Accountability. Specific data producers, computer users, and computer center staff are assigned explicit ownership or custodial accountability and usage rights for all data, data handling and processing capability, controls, and computer programs. This can be done by establishing policy; establishing meaning of ownership, usage, and custodianship; and requiring that forms be completed and logs made designating and recording such accountability for data and programs and copies of them in all locations and for specified times. For example, one organization has a set of booklets for each data activity area--stating ownership, usage, custodial, and control requirements. Another organization has this information as part of its policy manual. Accountability for assets is basic to their security. Accountability assignments also make clear who is responsible and accountable for each control and its effectiveness and overall adequacy of protection.

Classification of Data File and Program Name. Names for data files and computer programs are necessary for computer program development and documentation. They are also necessary for job setup and in some cases for computer operation. However, file and program names need not be known by those people who are in a transaction relationship with the computer system and not concerned with programming of computer applications. Therefore, a different set of terminology, and naming of entities should be developed for documentation of users manuals and for transaction activities, especially those of a sensitive nature. The least-privilege or need-to-know principle significantly reduces the exposure of sensitive assets. Separation of duties should also include the separation of information.

Compliance with Laws and Regulations. A statement regarding the new or modified system's compliance with relevant laws and regulations should be provided in requirements and specifications. Direct quotes from laws and regulations regarding ADP security and privacy applying within a legal jurisdiction, or those that may apply, should be included.

This provides management with increased assurance that an application system is in compliance with relevant laws and regulations, thereby reducing the chances that management liability and other sanctions might be applied. However, unless reviewed by a lawyer or some other knowledgeable person and compliance is assured by audit, control can become merely a perfunctory piece of paperwork where the blanks are filled in regardless of compliance with laws and regulations.

- **LABELS**

  While not required for C2 level of protection, the Orange Book states that "sensitivity labels associated with each subject and storage object under its control (e.g., process, file, segment, device) shall be maintained by the computer system. These labels shall be used as the basis for mandatory access control decisions. In order to import non-labeled data, the computer system shall request and receive from an authorized user the security level of the data, and all such actions shall be auditable by the computer system."

  Classification Printed on Media. Sensitive and valuable documents have a classification (e.g., SECRET, CONFIDENTIAL, FOUO, PRIVACY ACT, etc.) or an explicit warning--indicating that the information is the property of a certain organization, that it should be handled according to special criteria, that it is not to be used for certain purposes, etc. One site chose to print "CONFIDENTIAL" in the middle of the page; although this made reading a bit more difficult, it prevented people from cropping and photocopying the record--removing any indication that it was confidential. Another approach is to have the computer print appropriate words on only sensitive output. This has the advantage of warning display terminal users that the information should be specially treated. Policies and procedures should also be written.

This control reduces ambiguity associated with the use and dissemination of sensitive information, provides concrete evidence that steps were taken to control information, and can be used to control use of proprietary software. Likelihood of privacy violation can to some extent be avoided or lessened. Use of copyright or trademark laws may reduce unauthorized distribution and usage of sensitive information.

- **LABELING HUMAN-READABLE OUTPUT**

  The Orange Book states that "the ADP system administrator shall be able to specify the printable label names associated with exported sensitivity labels. The computer system shall mark the beginning and end of all human-readable, paged, hardcopy output (e.g., line printer output) with human-readable sensitivity labels that properly represent the overall sensitivity of the output or that properly represent the sensitivity of the information on that page. The computer system shall, by default and in an appropriate manner, mark other forms of human-readable output (e.g., maps, charts, graphics) with human-readable sensitivity labels that properly represent the sensitivity of the output. Any override of these marking defaults shall be auditable by the computer system."

Data Classification Levels. Data may be sensitive at different security levels to produce cost savings and effectiveness of applying controls--consistent with various levels of data sensitivity. Some organizations maintain the same level of security for all data, believing that making exceptions is too costly. Other organizations may have only small amounts of data of a highly sensitive nature and find that applying special controls to the small amount of data is cost-effective. When data are sensitive, they may be identified in two or more levels, often referred to as general information, confidential information, secret information and other higher levels of classification named according to the functional use of the data, such as trade secret data, unreported financial performance, etc.

Separate security treatment of data at different levels of security can result in control cost savings when the volume and concentration of sensitive data warrant special treatment. Otherwise, savings can be achieved by reducing control exceptions.

Keeping Security Reports Confidential. Computer security requires the use and filing of numerous reports, including results of security reviews, audits, exception reports, documentation of loss incidence, documentation of controls, control installation and maintenance, and personnel information. These reports are extremely sensitive and should be protected to the same degree as the highest level of information classification within the organization. A clean desk policy should be maintained in the security and audit offices. All security documents should be physically locked in sturdy cabinets. Computer-readable files should be secured separately from other physically stored files and should have high-level access protection when stored in a computer. The security function in an organization sets an example for the rest of the organization by appropriately caring for confidential information.

- **EXPORTATION OF LABELED INFORMATION**

   The Orange Book states that the "computer system shall designate each communication channel and I/O device as either single-level or multi-level. Any change in this designation shall be done manually and shall be auditable by the computer system. The computer system shall maintain and be able to audit any change in the security level or levels associated with a communication channel or I/O device."

   Courier Trustworthiness and Identification. Couriers are frequently used to distribute computer output reports to computer users. Couriers should be especially trustworthy, have a background investigation similar to that for computer operators, and be bonded. A new courier should be personally introduced to all those persons to whom he or she will be delivering computer output and to all persons from whom he will be receiving materials for delivery. Couriers should be required to use signed receipts for all transported reports. Couriers should be required to keep all reports in their personal possession in properly locked or controlled containers. All users should be informed immediately upon the termination of any couriers delivering or picking up reports. Couriers should carry special identification to show that they are authorized to function in claimed capacities. Telephone calls in advance of delivery of highly sensitive reports should be made to recipients of those reports.

The C-TEP team would suggest that the Security Administrator follow anyone picking up a sensitive batch run tape from the computer room. Their activities should be compared to receipt of tape at both pick-up and drop-off sites. In lieu of a contracted courier service, this procedure would also apply to employees from other organizations carrying a sensitive tape between sites.

- **CONFIGURATION MANAGEMENT**

    The Orange Book states that "during development and maintenance of the computer system, a configuration management system shall be in place that maintains control of changes to the descriptive top-level specifications, other design data, implementation documentation, source code, the running version of the object code, and test fixtures and documentation. The configuration management system shall assure a consistent mapping among all documentation and code associated with the current version of the computer system. Tools shall be provided for generation of a new version of the computer system from source code. Also available shall be tools for comparing a newly generated version with the previous version in order to ascertain that only the intended changes have been made in the code that will actually be used as a new version of the computer system."

    Configuration Control. Poor security procedures may permit the system to be configured improperly. This could lead to the unintentional storing of sensitive data on non-sensitive devices or the sending of sensitive data to a remote terminal that should have been disconnected. Both hardware and software configuration management is necessary to permit reasonable and continual verification that the computer system functions as intended. Modular design provides a means of isolating to a large extent the security features, thus minimizing the number of interactions between them and other operations. Establishing a system of configuration control affords the methodology for thorough analysis and testing of any system changes before implementation, which is advisable to protect against undesirable effects on the system's security. After the system is operational, configuration control of both hardware and software serves to verify that undetected changes have not taken place.

The C-TEP team would suggest that the Security Administrator check to see that a configuration control checklist has been established. This checklist should contain detailed procedures for connecting the individual sensitive processing system components together into the specific system configuration to be employed during each period. These procedures include setting all hardware switches, powering up and down of each device, loading the standard software and firmware for the configuration system, system operating procedures, and shutdown and restart procedures. Strict adherence to the established procedures is essential for overall system security. To insure that the procedures are followed, it is desirable that two people verify the new configuration.

The cost of developing a configuration control checklist is principally administrative. The cost of following this checklist is the time for the console operator and another person to verify the actual configuration against the checklist.

Computer Program Quality Assurance. A testing or quality control group should independently test and examine computer programs and related documentation to ensure the integrity of program products before production use. This activity is best authorized by software development management or by the quality assurance or test department. Excessively formal program development standards should be avoided. Basic life-cycle procedures should be established before more elaborate practices are required. However, compliance with the established standards and procedures should be strongly enforced. A consistent compliance with good controls design offsets computer programmers' resistance to independent observation of their work.

The C-TEP team would suggest that the Security Administrator independently test and examine computer programs and related documentation to ensure their integrity.

Responsibilities for Application Program Controls. The inclusion of controls in application programs should be explicitly ensured and documented--starting with design requirements and continuing through specifications development, production, and maintenance stages. The responsibility for adequacy and types of controls should be shared among ADP auditors, systems analysts, computer programmers, users, and data owners. Explicit documentation of controls is essential to ensure completion of their implementation and testing.

Operational procedures should be developed to carry out the intent of the controls, and to ensure their integrity during system change and maintenance.

It is difficult to explicitly document all application program controls. However, establishing procedures to ensure that controls are adequate and included in applications provides assurance that applications will be adequately controlled.

Auditors' participation in design requirements and post implementation testing for compliance with specifications should be monitored by the Security Administrator.

Vendor-supplied Program Integrity. To the greatest extent possible and practical, vendor-supplied computer programs should be used without modification. Many new vendor-supplied computer programs have been developed with controls and integrity build into them. Any modifications to these programs could compromise the built-in capabilities. Desired changes to the programs should be obtained from the vendor as standard program updates. This control is a means of preserving the security and integrity built into vendor-supplied computer programs. It is also a means of holding vendors responsible for any deficiencies in the programs.

The C-TEP team would suggest that the Security Administrator check to see if this control will reduce the frequency of changes to computer programs, facilitating direct code comparison of production programs with master backup copies. This should be done periodically to ensure that management policy is followed in restricting modification of vendor-supplied computer programs.

Confirmation of Receipt of Media. The confirmation process consists of verification of receipt of documents. Confirmations of delivery can be made by obtaining master files of names of input/output documents and their addressees, performing a selection of a sample of addressees by running the master file on a computer separate from the production computer or at least at a time different from normal production work. Confirmation notices and copies of the documents are then sent to the addressees to confirm that the documents are correct and that they received the documents as expected. Confirmation of smaller volumes of documents can be easily done on a manual basis. Receipt forms are used by recipients of particularly sensitive documents and returned to the sender to confirm correct report distribution and encourage accountability.

This control is used as an audit tool. The C-TEP team would suggest that the Security Administrator review the number and nature of confirmation-related activities for cost and benefits. The Security Administrator should also sample receipts and sensitive report deliveries to confirm correct procedures.

Correction and Maintenance of Production Run. In spite of implementation and strict enforcement of security controls and good maintenance of application and systems programs, emergencies arise that requires violation or overriding of many of these controls and practices. Occasionally, production programs will fail during production runs on the computer. This may happen on second and third shift, during periods of heavy production computer activity. If a failure occurs in a critical application production run, it is frequently necessary to call upon knowledgeable programmers to discover the problem, make a change in the production computer program, make changes in input data, or make decisions about alternative solutions (e.g., reruns using previous versions of the production program). When such emergency events occur, all necessary and expedient measures should be taken, including physical access of programmers to computer and production areas, access by such programmers to data files and production programs, correction of production programs, and ad hoc instructions to operations staff.

During any of these activities, it is necessary for a trusted individual in computer application production work to record all of the events as they occur or shortly thereafter. Following the termination of the emergency, programmers should be required to make the necessary permanent changes that may have been made on a temporary basis during the emergency and document the emergency actions. This usually requires updating and testing production programs and the normal process of introducing tested/updated programs for production use.

After an emergency and before permanent corrections have been made, the production application program should be treated in a "suspicious" mode of operation, requiring increased levels of observance by users, production staff managers, and possibly ADP auditors. These extra efforts should continue until confidence has been built up in the production activities through acceptable experience.

The C-TEP team would suggest that the Security Administrator create a theoretical situation in which an emergency override will take place. The Security Administrator should oversee the emergency procedures and production work which should take place in patching a sensitive computer program.

Limited Use of System Utility Programs. Most computer installations have one or more system utility programs capable of overriding all or most computer system and application controls. In some computer installations, one such computer program is called Superzap. In one large DoD computer installation previously studied by the author, five such utility programs were found. These programs should be controlled by password or kept physically removed from the computer system and the program library and physically controlled so that they are available only to a limited number of authorized users.

Occasionally, if the programs are made available on-line, they can be protected by special passwords required for their use. Changing the name or password frequently is another way to better safeguard these on-line programs. Limitations of availability of system utility programs forces programmers to use more accepted means of accomplishing their purposes that can be more safely done under the controls of the system.

Tape and Disk Management. A tape and disk management system can be used to keep track of all tapes and disks using a serial number appearing on the tape reel or disk. Serial numbers may contain storage rack location information as well as an identification number. Operators handling the tapes or disks do not know the contents of the tapes because the identity of the data set owner, creation and update dates, data set names, and like information is recorded only on internal (machine readable) labels. The software package for managing tapes and disks contains an index of serial numbers and the corresponding label information. An up-to-date copy of the index, relating serial numbers and tape and disk information, is maintained at off-site storage location(s).

This control provides operators with no more information than is necessary to do their jobs, thus preventing potential abusive acts that were made possible because these data were available to the operators. Operators are presented only with a request to mount or dismount certain tapes based on provided serial numbers. Disks should always be secured. A tape and disk management system can be used to monitor operator performance as well as to control the tape library. Persons in the tape library or machine room cannot learn the nature of the data on a tape simply by examining the reel. Disks can be kept in off-site storage using proper security methodology.

The C-TEP team would suggest that the Security Administrator trace the steps taken to obtain a tape from the Magnetic Media Library, mount and dismount the tape reel, etc.,--from initiation of a request to actual performance of the operator to return of the tape to Magnetic Media Library. The Security Administrator should also examine the data available to the operator to determine if confidentiality is not lessened by unwarranted exposure. The Security Administrator should also inspect the storage of disks at the sites.

Contingency Recovery Equipment Replacement. Sensitive processing commitments should be obtained in writing from computer equipment and supplies vendors to replace critical equipment and supplies within a specified period of time following a contingency loss. Some vendors will commit to replacement of their products within a reasonable period of time and will specify that period of time as a commitment. For example, in one computer installation a vendor agreed to replace a central processor within 5 days and a second processor, if necessary, within 10 days. The paper forms supplier agreed to deliver a two-week supply of all special forms in the same time frame. In contrast, other vendors would not guarantee replacement times but would only indicate that best efforts would be provided. This usually means that the next available equipment within the vendor company inventory would be provided with a priority over other normal product deliveries. Emergency ordering procedures should be established as part of a contingency recovery plan. Vendor commitments provide a means of planning alternative data processing until equipment and new computing capabilities have been restored.

The C-TEP team would suggest that the Security Administrator confirm the validity of agreements to be sure that they are still in effect. Commitment periods should be checked relative to disaster recovery plans with RO's, etc.

Minimizing Copies of Sensitive Data Files and Reports. The number of copies of sensitive tape, disk, or paper files should be minimized. Destruction dates should be specified and destruction instructions followed. It may be advisable to destroy most paper copies of files on the basis that the information can be retrieved and reprinted from computer media when necessary. This is based on the concept that files stored in computer systems and computer media are generally often more secure than on paper. Normal backup procedures often require that several copies of computer media files be made and stored at different sites. However, some files may be so sensitive that numerous copies in different locations may contribute to their exposure. As many as 20 to 30 copies of computer-stored files may be produced in a single year in a large computer installation. The organization primarily accountable for highly sensitive information should have control and logs of all copies and their locations. Adequate backup should be balanced with the exposure danger of multiple copies and backup procedures.

The C-TEP team would suggest that the Security Administrator make a selective examination of storage areas looking for sensitive records and comparing them to others for possible duplication.

Automation of Computer Operations. Computer operations should be made as automatic as possible, using such capabilities as production, program and test program libraries, automatic tape library management, and computer operator activity logging. This reduction of manual procedures generally results in improved control of computer operations activities. Reduction of staff reduces exposure to accidental or intentionally caused loss, and provides motivation to use automated operations packages beyond other considerations of cost-effectiveness.

- **DISASTER RECOVERY PLANNING, TESTING AND EVALUATING**

  Contingency and Recovery Funds. The computer center should be assured of readily available emergency funds for contingencies and recovery from terrorist attacks. Leasing equipment, which will be replaced by the vendor, if damaged or otherwise lost, may not be the only solution.

  The C-TEP team would suggest that the Security Administrator determine what funds can be made available if needed and what equipment hardware, software, etc) is owned, rather than leased, by the Security Administrator's organization.

  Data File and Program Back-up. The current form of every data file that may be needed in the future should be copied at the time of its creation and the copy should be stored at a remote, safe location for operational recovery purposes. It may be advisable to store several copies, one immediately available in the computer center, another available some short distance away, and a third archived at some remote distance for longer term storage. Periodically updated data files should be cycled from the immediate site to the local site to the remote site by data file generations (father, grandfather, etc.). In addition, copies of the computer programs necessary to process the backed-up data files, documentation of the programs, computer operation instructions, and a supply of special printed forms necessary for production running of the programs should also be stored at a remote, safe location. This hierarchical arrangement of backup data files provides for convenient restarting of production runs in case of damaged or missing files, more serious problems that could result in loss of local backup data files can be resolved by using copies of remote backup data files. When a backup file is returned to the computer center for use, there should be assurance that it is also backed up safely with another copy.

Defensive depth of backup provides significant increase in assurance of recovery that addresses small as well as large contingencies. Recovery from backup files is commonly done under abnormal conditions that usually accompany recovery efforts. These conditions increase the likelihood of loss of the backup files. Therefore, it is important to have at least secondary backup in addition to primary backup files.

The C-TEP team would suggest that the Security Administrator insist upon an actual demonstration of recovery from the backup level. Inspection of backup sites should also be conducted to ensure their secure status.

Disaster Recovery. The mainframe computer sites and remote sensitive processing sites should have a written disaster recovery plan and a recovery management team. Primary and backup managers should be assigned specific responsibilities for each aspect of recovery from all types of partial or complete disasters. Each aspect of the disaster recovery plan should have assigned a specific individual responsible for its execution. Separate individuals should be assigned to coordination, systems support, hardware recovery, facilities, administration, scheduling, communications, documentation and supplies, backup data files and security recovery funding, personnel, historical and recording of events. Priority processing needs of all time-dependent applications to be recovered after a disaster should be identified. This requires that all computer users (or someone acting on behalf of the users) specify the importance of their computer applications, processing requirements, and alternative means of processing, and consequences of failure to process. Data processing management is responsible for meeting the critical needs of computer users in the best interests of the organization. Priorities will assist in the scheduling of processing when it is restored.

A designated person should provide liaison with users informing them of special needs and the status of processing of their work. A detailed history of the recovery process should be documented and recovery activity verbally reported during the recovery process. After recovery, the historical documentation should be analyzed to determine how future contingencies may be better handled and to handle insurance claims recovery and any litigation that may follow a disaster. Every job function should be analyzed relative to its performance during and prior to a disaster. Measures of criticality and priority of functions should be determined and documented in the plan.

Flexibility in plans facilitates meeting a wide range of contingencies. A documented recovery plan provides for a means of practicing and testing all recovery procedures. Potential hacker or terrorist threats that can provide a means of adding controls to reduce risk may be identified. Prioritizing applications provides users with perspective on the importance of better applications recovery needs. Application of limited data processing resources can be more effectively planned. Communication among recovery managers helps ensure smooth and minimum cost recovery. Documentation of recovery activities encourages responsibilities and accountability among managers and workers. Job function analysis facilitates management's quick mobilization of critical personnel and resources in the event of a disaster. Management can more easily and effectively assign work to employees during recovery. A disaster plan reduces the likelihood of confusion. Use of a disaster recovery contact list provides for speedy notification of vendors, suppliers, and customers who can take appropriate action to assist or reduce loss.

The C-TEP team would suggest that the Security Administrator study all organizational disaster recovery plans to ensure that they are current. Proof of testing plans should be documented and reported. Scenarios of possible terrorist actions should be generated and theoretically played against the disaster recovery plans to ensure their adequacy. Application priorities should be verified through the Security Administrator for the audit of specific functions of an organization dependent on computer services. Examination of historical documentation recovery experience should be performed to note any changes necessary in disaster recovery planning for the future.

Electrical Equipment Protection. Every item of computing equipment that is separately powered should have a separate circuit breaker in the electrical supply for that equipment. Alternatively, equipment may be supplied with other protective mechanisms from power failures or other electrical anomalies. Circuit breakers should be clearly labeled for manual activation. The locations of all circuit breakers should be documented and available in disaster and recovery plans.

Individual devices can fail and be switched off without having to cut power to other devices. Failures can be localized as well as more readily detected. Device configurations can be changed more readily, avoiding excessive time in diagnosing electrical problems and reconfiguring electrical systems to suit new equipment setups.

Electrical Power Shutdown and Recovery. Emergency master power-off switches should be located next to each emergency exit door. The switches should be clearly identified, and easily read signs should be posted giving instructions for use of the switches. Activation of any of these switches should be followed with reports documenting the circumstances and persons responsible for their use. Alternative power supplies should be available when data processing needs justify continuous operations, and they should be tested on a periodic basis. The power supply should be used during the test for a sufficiently long period of time to ensure sustained operation under emergency conditions.

Easily identified power-off switches are valuable for firemen, rescue workers, and others in the event of emergencies. Testing facilitates preventive maintenance work and familiarizes staff with emergency procedures. Redundancies in alternative power supplies increase assurance of emergency recoveries.

- **SECURITY AWARENESS AND TRAINING**

  Security Training. Security training is of the utmost importance if only to remind personnel that they are handling sensitive data, etc.

  In compliance with the Computer Security Act of 1987, the C-TEP team may well find that the computer center has provided the required mandatory security awareness and training: covering technical, administrative, personnel, and physical security areas.

  Security Administrator. An organization has sufficient computer security resources to justify an individual as a full-time Security Administrator. The Security Administrator should ideally report to the overall security department covering the entire organization. This provides proper scope of responsibility for information and its movement throughout the organization. For practical purposes the Security Administrator often functions within the computer department. Job descriptions are highly variable; examples may be obtained from many organizations with established computer security officers. A Security Administrator provides a focus for the formal development of a computer security program.

- **COMMUNICATIONS SECURITY**

  Communication Lines and Links. It is possible to tap or monitor surreptitiously a data communication line or link. Any data passed along the communications lines or links are susceptible to hostile interception or manipulation.

  Transmissions and communication lines and links between components of the system should be secured at a level appropriate for the material to be transmitted. In the case of sensitive material, the protections for secure communication lines or links can be found as guides published by the Department of Defense (DoD). One such publication is DoD Military Handbook #232 on RED/BLACK criteria of communication lines and links. Approved cryptography can also be used to protect information against a variety of threats. For secure electrical transmission of unencrypted information, when relatively short distances and controlled areas are involved, a Protected Distribution System (PDS) may be used as an alternative to cryptography. For sensitive information or Privacy Act data, secure transmission is not mandated. However, during transmission some form of security should be provided, especially for sensitive business data.

- **MICROCOMPUTER SECURITY**

  Hardware Concerns. The C-TEP team, before reviewing the data and software security issues surrounding microcomputers and terminals linked to networks, should review the hardware concerns of physical access, potential for theft, environmental damage, lack of magnetic media protection, and the lack of built-in security mechanisms common with the microcomputer environment.

  The C-TEP team may find that access to microcomputers is normally limited to authorized users. While evidence will probably exist that untrained individuals or malicious acts may have damaged a small percentage of terminals, the necessary precautions should be in force.

The C-TEP team will probably find some high-value computer items to be unaccountable. While short of inspecting everything that leaves the building, it is suggested that rooms be secured at the end of the working day and that lock-down devices be installed to secure the terminals to a table or desk.

Microcomputers are handled more than the automated equipment in the main computer room and are thus more suspect to damage. They are sensitive to the quality of electrical power and it is suggested that surge protectors be used. Also, while a site may not know the electrical line configuration in the building, it is recommended that microcomputers not be plugged into the same electrical box that is also providing power to the coffee maker, refrigerator, or other heavy electrical use appliances.

The other potential for environmental damage is static electricity. It is suggested that an anti-static spray be used to minimize this danger.

Particular attention should be given to the protection of magnetic media, whether floppy disks or internal rigid disks. The Security Administrator should post a sign or otherwise publicize the fact that disks need to be handled with care; always stored in their protective jackets, protected from bending, stored within an acceptable temperature range, etc.

Lastly, a major security weakness of microcomputers is that they lack built-in hardware security mechanisms such as memory protection features, multiple processor states, or privileged instructions. It is virtually impossible to prevent users from accessing the operating system and thereby circumventing any intended security mechanisms. For example, any user could reformat the hard disk on the "c: drive" while thinking they are simply formatting a floppy on the "a: drive." It occurs more than what is acceptable. It is suggested that certain functions be removed from DOS (FORMAT, DISKCOPY, etc.) and that these functions be delegated to a central point within the organization.

Data Concerns. The information processed and stored at the microcomputer level is more easily accessed (potentially by unauthorized users) than that found on larger systems. The C-TEP team should look at labeling, the security of data media, data corruption, and data transmission.

Sensitive data resources must be clearly labeled. Sensitive data, especially those which could qualify for the AGENCY SENSITIVE or PRIVACY ACT label, should not be allowed to reside on the hard disk. All floppy disks should be labeled to indicate the sensitivity of the data on the disk. These floppy disks should be placed in a secure container or locking desk (if the user has the only key to the desk lock). Locking the disks in a diskette box is of no value as the entire box can be removed from the area. Also important is the daily use of back-ups of all important and sensitive data and their storage.

Because of the lack of hardware security features, the C-TEP team should insist that microcomputers cannot be trusted to prevent the corruption of data. For example, while in a sensitive WordPerfect document you decide to Block and Move a sensitive paragraph within the file. You then save that document and bring up another WordPerfect file that is not sensitive in nature. By using the Move command again you can duplicate the sensitive data left in memory from the previous file. Your non-sensitive file is now corrupted and now actually contains sensitive data. You may wish to delete that file from the floppy or hard disk; however, few users realize that deleting the file only removes the file name pointer and not the data. By using a software utilities package like Norton Utilities you can recall the file by just following the menu in the program.

Finally, transferring data to or from a mainframe environment should be carefully controlled and monitored. The microcomputer user must be held accountable for ensuring that sensitive data is transferred only to other computers designated to receive sensitive data. For example, a sensitive counter-terrorist report can be sent to everyone on the message handling address database if the person sending the file does not know how to send the message. If there is a question, the user should not proceed.

Software Concerns. Operating systems cannot be trusted since certain functions do not work as reasonably expected. For example, as mentioned earlier, the Erase or Delete command does not actually erase files--it merely releases the file space, leaving the data intact.

The C-TEP team would suggest that some type of user identification be used and that the Security Administrator make users aware of potential damage to their system due to software attacks--trapdoors, Trojan Horses, worms and viruses.

- **CERTIFICATION**

  __Certification.__ It would always be highly suggested by the C-TEP team that a certification process begin and be maintained by those ultimately responsible for the handling and security of the sensitive data. The certification begins when an ADP Security Handbook has been published and distributed. Included in the certification process is a workable Disaster Recovery Plan, an up-to-date Risk Assessment of the sites handling sensitive data, and other security items of interest.

  __Computer Security Management Committee.__ A high-level management committee should be organized to develop counter-terrorist security policies and oversee all security of information handling activities. The committee should be composed of management representatives from each part of the organization concerned with information processing. The committee would be responsible for coordinating computer security matters, reviewing the state of system security, ensuring the visibility of management's support of computer security throughout the organization, approving computer security reviews, receiving and accepting computer security review reports, and ensuring proper control interfaces among organization functions. Computer security reviews and recommendations for major controls should be made to and approved by this committee.

  The committee ensures that privacy and security are part of the overall information handling plan. The Steering Committee may be part of a larger activity within an organization having responsibility for the function of information resource management. For example, in one research and development organization an oversight council, made up of representatives from organizations that send and receive databases to and from the R&D organization was established. The council was charged with oversight responsibilities for the conduct and control of the R&D organization relative to the exchange of databases. Especially important are questions of individual privacy concerning the content of the databases. The objective is to prevent the loss of security support which could result from ineffective handling of sensitive information.

A Steering Committee visibly shows top management's dedication and support for security issues to the entire organization. Security activity is organized on a top-down basis. A committee that crosses organizational lines can better ensure the consistency of security across the interfaces and the consistency of attention to security in all information-processing related functions. The Steering Committee can consider security and privacy within the context of other issues confronting the organization. Policies and procedures can be more effectively enforced. The committee approach can avoid the control of computer security by technologists who tend to be limited to technical solutions to security problems.

CHAPTER 4: SUMMARY

"Thus far, organized terrorist groups have failed to focus on data processing facilities as a key to disruptive incidents." [Quoted in 1983][156]

"The masters of terror are fast learning that high-tech is the Achilles' heel of post-industrial society." [Quoted just four years later, in 1987]"[157]

This research paper has shown in detail that terrorists are becoming more intelligent and have already established a successful record in destroying computer centers and their data. The war against computer terrorism has escalated: what was once a simple matter of throwing bombs into computer centers has evolved into attacking computer systems electronically through the use of Trojan Horses, software bugs, worms and

---

[156]Belden Menkus, "Notes on Terrorism and Data Processing," Computers & Security, January 1983, 13.
[157]August Bequai, Techno-Crimes: The Computerization of Crime and Terrorism, (Lexington MA: Lexington Books, 1987).

viruses. The polymorphic virus, or "stealth" virus is one of the most destructive virus yet. Terrorist organizations and hostile intelligence groups have even been caught using hackers to do their electronic mayhem for them and to even break into sensitive computer databases to steal data. Most recently, terrorists have been discovered using computers to help them keep track of their own resources or their next potential kidnap victim.

Terrorists are becoming more intelligent and our computer resources now need to be made more safe from the determined actions of these intelligent terrorists. From a Security Administrator's standpoint, this book has shown that terrorist actions against computer resources does have historical precedence, and that the Security Administrator can fight this increasing threat by taking a proactive stance and implementing a Computer-Terrorism Evaluation Plan (C-TEP) such as the one offered in this book.

Index

Acronyms & Abbreviations

AD	Action Directe (Direct Action), a terrorist organization
ADP	Automated Data Processing
ADPE	ADP Equipment
AHU	Air Handling Unit
Al Fatah	An Arab terrorist organization
ASIS	American Society for Industrial Security
ASSIST	Automated Systems Security Incident Support Team
AT&T	American Telephone and Telegraph
BKA	The German Federal Criminal Investigation Department
CCC	Combatant Communist Cells (Cellules Communistes Combattantes)
CDC	Control Data Corporation
CIA	Central Intelligence Agency
CLODO	Comite Liquidant ou Detoumant les Ordinateurs (Committee on the Liquidation or Deterrence of Computers)
Compu-Terror	Computer Terrorism
CSIS	Georgetown University's Center for Strategic and International Studies in Washington, D.C.
C-TEP	Compu-Terror Evaluation Plan
DARPA	Defense Advanced Research Projects Agency
DDN	Defense Data Network
DIA	Defense Intelligence Agency
DINCOTE	Peruvian National Antiterrorist Directorate
DOD	Department of Defense
DP	Data Processing
EFTS	Electronic Funds Transfer System
EMP-T	ElectroMagnetic Pulse Transformer bomb

FALN	Fuerzas Armadas de Liberacion Nacional, a Cuban-backed Puerto Rican terrorist organization
FBI	Federal Bureau of Investigation
FBIS	Foreign Broadcast Information Service
FOIA	Freedom of Information Act
FOUO	For Official Use Only
GAO	Government Accounting Office
GMT	Greenwich Mean Time, also known as zulu time, now called UTC for Coordinated Universal Time
HERF	High Energy Radio Frequency gun
IBM	International Business Machines Corporation
IEEE	Institute of Electrical and Electronics Engineers
IFIP	International Federation for Information Processing
Inter.Pact	International Partnership Against Computer Terrorism
IRA	Irish Republican Army
ITT	International Telephone and Telegraph
KGB	Komitet Gosudarstvennoye Bezopastnosti, the State Security Committee of the former Soviet Union
LABLN	Union of Basque Patriotic Workers, the labor arm of the radical Basque Party
MAN	The West German company Maschinenfabrick Ausburg-Nuernberg (MAN)
MIT	Massachusetts Institute of Technology
MML	Magnetic Media Library
MRTA	Peruvian Movimento Revolucionario Tupac Amaru, also known as the Tupac Amaru Revolutionary Movement
NAC	National Agency Check
NASA	National Aeronautics and Space Administration
NATO	North Atlantic Treaty Organization
NCAVC	The FBI's National Center for the Analysis of Violent Crime
NCR	National Cash Register Company
NORAD	North American Air Defense Command
NPA	New People's Army, the armed wing of the outlawed Communist Party of the Philippines
PDS	Protected Distribution System
PFLP	Popular Front for the Liberation of Palestine
PIOS	Personen, Institutionen, Objekte, Sachen (Persons, Institutions, Movable and Immovable Objects)

RAF	Red Army Faction, a West German terrorist organization
RISOS	Research in Secure Operating Systems
SDI	Strategic Defense Initiative
SDS	Students for a Democratic Society
VMM	Virtual Machine Monitor

Bibliography

America's Hidden Vulnerabilities. (Washington, D.C.: Georgetown University's Center for Strategic and International Studies (CSIS), October 1985).

Arkin, Stanley S., et al. Prevention and Prosecution of Computer and High Technology Crime. (New York, Matthew Bender & Co., 1992).

The Atlanta Journal and Constitution. "West German Attack Tied to Pro-Terrorists." (13 April 1989).

Automated Systems Security--Federal Agencies Should Strengthen Safeguards Over Personal and Other Sensitive Data. (Washington, D.C.: General Accounting Office, Government Printing Office, 23 January 1979).

Aviation Week & Space Technology. "Washington Roundup." (25 November 1991).

Bartimo, Jim. "Terrorism Vexing International DP Crime Experts." ComputerWorld. (12 July 1982).

Baskerville, Richard. Designing Information Systems Security. (New York: John Wiley & Sons, 1988).

Bates, Tom. Rads: The 1970 Bombing of the Army Math Research Center at the University of Wisconsin and its Aftermath. (New York: HarperCollins Publishers, 1992).

Beadsmoore, Michael. "Terrorism in the Information Age: A Recipe for Disaster?" Computerworld. (7 July 1986).

Bennett, Scott. "Viewpoints: The Growth of Terrorism." Dallas Morning News. (11 January 1990).

Bequai, August. How To Prevent Computer Crimes: A Guide for Managers. (New York: John Wiley & Sons, 1983).

_____. Techno-Crimes: The Computerization of Crime and Terrorism. (Lexington, MA: Lexington Books, 1987).

Bloombecker, Jay, ed. Introduction to Computer Crime. (Los Angeles, CA: National Center for Computer Crime Data, 1985).

Boorman, Scott A. and Paul R. Levitt. "Deadly Bugs." Chicago Tribune. (3 May 1987).

Brushweiler, Wallace S., Sr. "Computers as Targets of Transnational Terrorism." Computer Security. (North Holland: Elsevier Science Publishers), 1985.

Burger, Ralf. Computer Viruses: A High-Tech Disease, (Grand Rapids, MI: Abacus, 1988).

Clark, Richard C. Technological Terrorism. (Old Greenwich, CT: Devin-Adair Company, 1980).

Computer Weekly. "Bomb Attacks on French Centres." (11 December 1980).

Conner, Michael. Terrorism: Its Goals, Its Targets, Its Methods, The Solution. (Boulder, CO: Paladin Press, 1987).

Cooper, James Arlin. Computer and Communications Security: Strategies for the 1990s. (New York: McGraw-Hill, 1989).

Culnan, Mary. "Electronic Terrorism: How Can We Fight It?" The Atlanta Journal and Constitution. (13 April 1989).

Dallas Morning News. "Army Captures Hit Squad Chiefs in Columbia." (10 September 1989).

_____. "Probe Targets Klan; Tax, Rights Inquiry Includes Skinheads." (2 July 1990).

Datapro Research Corporation. "Terrorism's Threat to Information Processing." (July 1986).

David, Thomas. "Pentagon's Loss of Computer Control Opens Access to Data for Soviets." New York City Tribune. (22 January 1988).

Defense Security Institute. Soviet Acquisition of Militarily Significant Western Technology: An Update. (Washington, D.C.: Defense Security Institute), September 1985.

Dickson, David. "Animal Rightists Claim Bomb Blast." Science. (3 March 1989).

Directory of American Firms Operating in Foreign Countries. (New York: World Trade Academy Press, Volume I, 11th Edition, 1987).

Dobson, Christopher and Ronald Payne. Counterattack: The West's Battle Against the Terrorists. (New York: Facts on File, Inc., 1982).

Dotto, Lydia. "The New Computer Criminals." Atlas World Press Review. (August 1979).

Drogin, Bob. "Aquino Touts Victory Over Communists But Clashes Raise Doubts That Government Has Beaten Insurgency."

The Los Angeles Times. (12 March 1992).

Ecodefense: A Field Guide to Monkeywrenching, (Earth First! Publishers, 2nd edition).

Fischer, Dr. Lynn F. "The Threat to Automated Systems." Security Awareness Bulletin. Department of Defense Security Institute, Richmond, VA. (September 1991).

Foreign Broadcast Information Service (FBIS). "Government Computer Destroyed in Bomb Explosion." (13 October 1984).

_____. "Research Center Damaged in Bomb Explosion." (15 October 1984).

_____. "Bomb Damages Decoding Computer Plant in Bavaria." (13 April 1987).

_____. "Bomb Explodes Near Government Palace; More Attacks Reported." (14 May 1992).

_____. "Update on Anti-Terrorist Operations in the Basque Country." (14 May 1992).

_____. "Regional Guerrilla Activities 17-27 May." (29 May 1992).

_____. "Roundup of Terrorist Activities." (5 June 1992).

_____. "Durban Bomb Fatality at Computer Center." (2 October 1990).

Fites, Philip, Peter Johnston and Martin Kratz, The Computer Virus Crisis, (New York: Van Nostrand Reinhold, 1989).

The Futurist. "Terrorism and Computers." (January-February 1988).

Gertz, Bill. "Hackers' Success Worries Pentagon." Washington Times. (19 April 1988).

Harry, M. The Computer Underground: Computer Hacking, Crashing, Pirating and Phreaking. (Port Townsend, WA: Loompanics Unlimited Press).

Heather, Randall. Terrorism, "Active Measures", and SDI, (Toronto, Canada: The Mackenzie Institute for the Study of Terrorism, Revolution and Propaganda, 1987).

Henderson, Breck W. "Experts Say Total Security Program Needed to Counter Terrorist Threat." Aviation Week & Space Technology, (20 November 1989).

Higgins, Mike. "Polymorphic Viruses (Automated Systems Security Incident Support Team (ASSIST) 92-38)." Defense Data Network (DDN), undated.

Hoffman, L. "Impacts of Information System Vulnerabilities on Society." NCC Conference Proceedings. (Arlington, VA: AFIPS Press, 1982).

Hosinski, Joan M. "U.S. Said to Be Vulnerable in Information War." Government Computer News. (7 August 1989).

Hsaio, Kerr and Madnick. Computer Security. (New York: Academic Press, 1979).

Icove, David J. "Modeling the Threat." A committee report presented to the Department of Defense Invitational Workshop on Computer Security Incident Response, Carnegie-Mellon University Software Engineering Institute, Pittsburgh, PA, July 31-August 1, 1989.

_____. "Keeping Computers Safe." Security Management. (December 1991).

International Terrorism: A Chronology, 1968-1974. (Santa Monica, CA: The Rand Corporation, March 1975).

Jenish, D'Arcy. "A Terrorist Virus: Michelangelo Stirs Fears of Future Shocks." MacLean's. (16 March 1992).

Jenkins, Brian. "Defending Your Data." Government Executive. (October 1991).

Johnson, John. "'Dark Side' Hacker Seen as 'Electronic Terrorist'." Los Angeles Times. (8 January 1989).

Kupperman, Robert H. and Darrell M. Trent, eds. <u>Terrorism: Threat, Reality, Response</u>. (Standford, CA, Hoover Institution Press, 1979).

Lamb, John and James Etheridge. "DP: The Terror Target." <u>Datamation</u>. (1 February 1986).

Laquer, Walter and Yonah Alexander. <u>The Terrorism Reader: The Essential Source Book on Political Violence Both Past and Present</u>. (New York: Meridian Book, 1987).

Livingstone, Neil C. <u>The War Against Terrorism</u>. (Lexington, MA: Lexington Books, 1982).

_____. <u>The Cult of Counterterrorism</u>, (Lexington, MA: Lexington Books, 1990).

Lloyd, Andrew. "DP: An Easy Target." <u>Datamation</u>. (1 June 1980).

Long, David E. <u>The Anatomy of Terrorism</u>. (New York: The Free Press, 1990).

<u>Los Angeles Times</u>. "The World." (3 September 1985).

Markoff, John. "Top Secret and Vulnerable: 'Unguarded Doors' in U.S. Computers Disturb Experts." <u>New York Times</u>. (25 April 1988).

Martin, James. <u>Security, Accuracy and Privacy in Computer Systems</u>. (New York: Prentice Hall, Inc, 1973).

Menkus, Belden. "Notes on Terrorism and Data Processing." <u>Computers & Security</u>. (January 1983).

Moran, William B. <u>Covert Surveillance and Electronic Penetration</u>. (Port Townsend, WA: Loompanics Unlimited Press).

National Computer Security Association. <u>Computer Viruses</u>. (1 January 1991).

Norman, Adrian R.D. <u>Computer Insecurity</u>. (New York: Chapman and Hall, 1985).

O'Connor, Rory J. "Army Searches For New Weapon: Computer Virus." <u>Philadelphia Inquirer</u>. (7 May 1990).

Ognibene, Peter J. "America the Vulnerable." <u>Los Angeles Times</u>. (16 January 1991).

Orlandi, Eugenio. "Data Processing Security and Terrorism." A paper given at the Second International Federation for Information Processing (IFIP) International Conference on Computer Security, Toronto, Canada, 10-12 September, 1984.

Parker, Donn B. <u>Manager's Guide to Computer Security</u>. (Reston, VA: Reston Publishing Co., Inc., 1981).

Pollak, R. "Implications of International Terrorism on Security of Information Systems." <u>Proceedings of IEEE INFOCOM 83</u>. (New York: IEEE, 1983).

Rawles, James W. "High-Technology Terrorism." <u>Defense Electronics</u>. (January 1990).

_____. "The Viral Threat." <u>Defense Electronics</u>. (February 1990).

Reuters Newswire. "Counter-intelligence Hilite." (17 February 1990).

_____. "Dutch Computer Hackers Leave Global Trail of Damage." (31 January 1992).

_____. "U.S. General Wants Ray Guns for Commandos." (5 May 1992).

Roberts, Ralph and Pamela Kane. Computer Security. (Greensboro, NC: Compute! Books, 1989).

Rowley, James. "Libyans Indicted in Pan Am Blast. Pair Reportedly Intelligence Officers." The Phoenix Gazette. (14 November 1991).

Rozen, Arnon and John Musacchio. "Computer Sites: Assessing the Threat." Security Management. (July 1988).

Santoro, Victor. Disruptive Terrorism. (Port Townsend, WA: Loompanics Unlimited, 1984).

Schmemann, Serge. "Computer Buffs Tapped NASA Files." The New York Times. (16 September 1987).

Schwartau, Winn. "Seven Weapons for the Well-Armed Computer Terrorist." Information Security Product News. (September/October 1991).

_____. Terminal Compromise. (New York: Inter.Pact Press, 1991).

Security Awareness Bulletin. "Real or Imagined? The Hostile Intelligence Threat to Computer Systems." Defense Investigative Service/Defense Security Institute, June 1986.

Seiber, Ulrich. The International Handbook on Computer Crime: Computer-related Economic Crime and the Infringements of Privacy. (New York: John Wiley & Sons, 1986).

Sitomer, Curtis J. "Crooks find computers useful; terrorists see vulnerable targets." The Christian Science Monitor. (4 December 1986).

Solomon, Alan. "Sneaking Past the Scanners: Stealth Viruses, Part II." Infosecurity News. (November/December 1992).

St. Petersburg Times. "Washington Digest." (6 December 1990).

Stoll, Clifford. The Cuckoo's Egg: Tracking a Spy Through a Maze of Computer Espionage. (New York: Doubleday, 1989).

Suplee, Curt and Evelyn Richards, "Computers Vulnerable, Panel Warns." The Washington Post. (6 December 1990).

Terrorist Group Profiles, (Washington, D.C.: Government Printing Office, 1988).

Time-Life, Computer Security, (Alexandria, VA: Time-Life Books).

USA Today (magazine). "Terrorism: Home-Grown Threat to U.S.?" (December 1989).

U.S. Army, Countering Terrorism on U.S. Army Installations. Technical Circular (TC) 19-16, April 1983.

Van Eck, W. "Electromagnetic Radiation from Video Display Units: An Eavesdropping Risk." Computers & Security. (1985).

Washington Times. "Hackers Steal SDI Information." (24 December 1990).

Whiteside, Thomas. Computer Capers: Tales of Electronic Thievery, Embezzlement, and Fraud. (New York: A Mentor Book, The New American Library, Inc. 1978).

Wilcox, Richard H. and Patrick J. Garrity, eds. America's Hidden Vulnerability: Crisis Management in a Society of Networks. (Washington, D.C.: The Center for Strategic and International Studies, Georgetown University. (October 1984).

About the Author

LCDR Douglas E. Campbell, Ph.D., (USNR-R, Ret.) was born on May 9, 1954 in Portsmouth, Virginia, and grew up as a Navy Brat, traveling all over the world. He graduated from Kenitra American High School, Kenitra, Morocco, in 1972 – his 13th school. He received his Bachelor of Science degree in Journalism from the University of Kansas on May 24, 1976 and the following day was commissioned as an Ensign in the United States Navy. He joined the U.S. Naval Reserve Program as an Intelligence Officer in 1980 and was transferred to the Retired Reserves as a Lieutenant Commander on 1 June 1999. Dr. Campbell received his Master of Science degree from the University of Southern California in Computer Systems Management in 1986 and his Doctor of Philosophy degree in Security Administration from Southwest University in New Orleans, LA, in 1993.

Dr. Campbell is president and CEO of Syneca Research Group, Inc., a veteran-owned small business incorporated in 1995 supporting several Government and commercial clients. He currently resides with his wife Trish in Southern Pines, NC.

Dr. Campbell's published books include:

+ *USS DORADO (SS-248): On Eternal Patrol* (ISBN 978-1-257-95155-0)
+ *Volume III: U.S. Navy, U.S. Marine Corps and U.S. Coast Guard Aircraft Lost During World War II-Listed by Aircraft Type* (ISBN 978-1-257-90689-5); eBook ISBN is 978-1-105-20089-2
+ *Volume II: U.S. Navy, U.S. Marine Corps and U.S. Coast Guard Aircraft Lost During World War II-Listed by Squadron* (ISBN 978-1-257-88139-0); eBook ISBN is 978-1-105-19671-3
+ *Volume I: U.S. Navy, U.S. Marine Corps and U.S. Coast Guard Aircraft Lost During World War II-Listed by Ship Attached* (ISBN 978-1-257-82232-4); eBook ISBN is 978-1-105-16346-3
+ *Building a Global Information Assurance Program* with Raymond J. Curts, Ph.D. (ISBN 0-8493-1368-6)
+ *Compu-terror: Computer Terrorism and Recovery from Disaster* (ASIN B00071D2XO)

www.ingramcontent.com/pod-product-compliance
Lightning Source LLC
Chambersburg PA
CBHW051237050326
40689CB00007B/953